MENDOCINO COAST

BIKE RIDES

Dedicated to my mom, Carolyn Harman Lorentzen, courageous spirit,
who would be out there riding if she still could.

Acknowledgments

I am most grateful to everyone who helped with this book. In particular, Rick Hemmings, Jiró Tulley and Jeff Stanford of Catch-a-Canoe & Bicycles, Too provided invaluable encouragement, support, feedback, mechanical tune-ups and prodding for this project, from beginning to end. Linda Richmond brought her talent and verve to the cover art. Beca LaFore provided invaluable guidance in map production. Thanks to Jim and Judy Tarbell, Jiró Tulley, Chris Maruna, Tom Flowerday and Liz Petersen for help with specific rides. And as always, to Liz, who did so much, in so many grand and small ways, to bring this book from vague idea to solid reality.

Thank you to Hal Slack, Tess Albin-Smith and John Griffen of Jackson State Forest, Peter Braudrick of Mendocino Area State Parks and Bruce Cann of BLM for contributing information and dialogue on rides in their respective domains.

MENDOCINO COAST BIKE RIDES

Road & Trail Rides
from Easy to Advanced

by
Bob Lorentzen

BORED FEET PUBLICATIONS
1996

© 1996 by Robert S. Lorentzen
First printing, June 1996
Printed in the United States of America on 85% recycled paper
Maps by CA Department of Forestry (used by permission), USGS,
    Beca LaFore (Ride #1 map) and Liz Petersen
Design by Liz Petersen, Petersen Graphics, Fort Bragg, CA
Cover art by Linda Richmond

Published by Bored Feet Publications
Post Office Box 1832
Mendocino, California 95460
(707) 964-6629

This book was produced entirely on a PowerMacintosh 7500, created from dos text files imported into Adobe Pagemaker 6.0, with maps and cover art scanned then brought to final form in Aldus Freehand and Adobe Photoshop. It went direct from computer to film. Way cool.

Publisher's Cataloging-in-Publication Data

Lorentzen, Bob
Mendocino coast bike rides: road and trail rides from easy to advanced/ by Bob Lorentzen.
pp. 168
ISBN 0-939431-11-4
1. Cycling-California-Mendocino County (Calif.)-Guide-books.
2. Mendocino County (Calif.)-Description and travel-Guide-books.
I. Title.

10 9 8 7 6 5 4 3 2 1

Contents

East of Fort Bragg — Heart of Jackson State Forest

North of Fort Bragg — Toward the Lost Coast

Navarro River, Anderson Valley & Comptche

The South Coast — Gualala, Point Arena, Manchester & Elk

Glossary

Appendix

About Bored Feet

What Kind of Ride are You Looking For?

Cross Reference Listing

Family Rides on Pavement (little or no vehicle traffic)

2. Russian Gulch Canyon & Headlands, *Option 1*
5. Fern Canyon to Pygmy Forest, *Option 1*
14. MacKerricher State Park, *Option 1*
33. Westport-Union Landing State Beach, *Option 1*
39. Anderson Valley, *Options 1 & 3*
40. Headwaters of South Fork Big River, *Option 1*
43. Point Arena Headlands, *Options 1 & 3*

Other Safe Family Rides (no highway)

1. Mendocino Headlands State Park
2. Russian Gulch Canyon & Headlands, *Options 2, 3 & 4*
3. Point Cabrillo to Caspar Beach, *Option 1*
5. Fern Canyon to Pygmy Forest, *Option 2*
6. Headwaters of Russian Gulch, *Options 1 & 2*
7. Railroad Gulch
8. Little Lake Road
12. Caspar Creek Watershed, *Option 1*
13. Caspar Creek Canyon, *Option 1*
14. MacKerricher State Park, *Options 2 & 3*
15. Pudding Creek
18. Hare Creek Canyon, *Options 1, 2 & 4*
19. Hare Creek Watershed
20. Pygmy Forest Reserve
23. North Slope, South Fork Noyo River
26. North Fork of South Fork Noyo River, *Option 1*
29. Headwaters, Little North Fork Big River, *Option 1*
34. Branscomb Valley
35. Sinkyone Wilderness State Park, Usal, *Options 1 & 2*

Other Safe Family Rides (no highway) — continued

37. Navarro Ridge, *Options 1, 2 & 3*
38. Navarro River at Hendy Woods, *Options 1 & 2*

Rides with Short Single Track Sections
(Some technical challenge)

6. Headwaters of Russian Gulch, *Option 1*
12. Caspar Creek Watershed, *Option 2*
18. Hare Creek Canyon, *Option 4*
19. Hare Creek Watershed, *Options 1 & 2*
20. Pygmy Forest Reserve, *Options 2 & 3*

Rides with More Than a Mile of Single Track
(More technical challenge)

6. Headwaters of Russian Gulch, *Option 3*
9. Manly Gulch
10. Railroad Gulch East Slope
16. Company Ranch to Jackass Pass
21. Bunker Gulch & Bunker Hill, *Option 3*
22. Camp One Loop
26. North Fork of South Fork Noyo River & Ridge Loop, *Options 2 & 3*
28. Berry Gulch, *Option 4*
32. Headwaters of North Fork Big River, *Options 2, 3 & 4*
36. Hidden Valley to Chemise Mountain

Most Challenging Rides
(* The toughest)

9. Manly Gulch
10. Railroad Gulch East Slope
17. Sherwood Ridge, *Options 2 & 3*
21. Bunker Gulch & Bunker Hill, *Option 3*
* 22. Camp One Loop, *Option 2*
* 26. North Fork of South Fork Noyo River & Ridge Loop, *Options 2 & 3*
* 28. Berry Gulch, *Option 4*
32. Headwaters of North Fork Big River, *Options 2, 3 & 4*
35. Sinkyone Wilderness State Park, Usal, *Option 4*
* 36. Hidden Valley to Chemise Mountain
40. Headwaters of South Fork Big River, *Option 2 (strenuous) & 3*
44. Mountain View Road, *Option 4*

Introduction

Finally! Over the many hundreds of miles I rode putting this guide together, at last I became one with my bike!

Not that I couldn't ride before — by age four I was a holy terror on training wheels. But somehow I'd never managed to ride enough, on the full variety of terrain, to be totally comfortable on two wheels — until the eleventh or twelfth scouting ride for this book, on my new mountain bike.

It was about the tenth mile of a 15-mile day on dirt. The final descent was steep and rough after an afternoon of big climbs and descents. Suddenly I fell into a groove, got loose, and connected with the machine. Heads up! Big rocks all over the track? I glided right through them. Hang loose! Loose dirt — the bike danced through it. Steep drop! Sit back, relax, go with the flow, eyes ahead, fingers on brakes.

It was so much fun I took a four-mile cool-down ride. Practicing my attack, coast and relax, charge and attack rhythms. Suddenly I wasn't a hiker on a bike, I was one with my machine, going with the flow, soaking it in, riding with rhythm and grace.

No way am I the hottest rider on dirt. I'm a novice and proud of it. Not sure you want to follow the tracks of a novice?

This book tells it like I found it. What's fun and what's terrifying, what's a grind and where to groove. You advanced riders may laugh — you might not need this book anyway. But if you weren't born on a bike, or if you're new to the neighborhood — and what a great big and beautiful 'hood the Mendocino Coast is! — I know the territory. I've been tromping local tracks and trails for twenty years.

Why did I suddenly decide to explore it on a bike? The guys at the bike shop knew I knew the countryside. They grabbed me and said "Lotsa people wanna know where to ride — it's the rage! Tell 'em where." So many people driving around with loaded bike racks, looking for the good rides. I saw a few places glutted with riders and so many tracks that seldom heard the mesh of gears.

I have selfish reasons too. I love this north coast redwood country and I like to see people discover its remote corners, to claim them for public access. I hate to see cyclists ride hiking trails through fragile terrain where bikes don't belong. So many good places to ride — why go trash the Jughandle Ecological Staircase or the fragile, botanically rich headlands?

I have one more reason — to encourage cyclists to ride responsibly. Don't go thrashing through mud holes — get off and walk your machine around them. Want to ride after a big storm? Find some lonesome pavement or a good, hard-packed gravel back road. Save the more sensitive spots for the dry season. Most likely you bikers will be traveling faster than any other humans on these tracks (barring motor vehicles), so keep heads up, eyes open, and brake for any walkers, horseback riders and four-legged creatures you encounter on your cruise. Enjoy!

How to Use This Book

The 46 main rides described in this book include 168 different OPTIONS, choices you can make to extend (or shorten) that outing. Within each chapter, Option 1 describes the easiest route, a ride with little or no highway riding. Options 2 through 5 cover rides longer and/or more difficult than the first Option. Each Option shows distance, elevation gain and loss, and how much vehicle traffic you're likely to encounter. Options are classified as easy, moderate, strenuous or advanced. Rides within each category vary considerably, so the Ride Notes give you the details. (Most loops described are more difficult in the opposite direction.)

The rides are organized by area, so you can quickly locate the rides nearest you. Each ride's DIRECTIONS TO STARTING POINT gives a precise description of how to get there from Highway One, 101 or 128. Most of the DIRECTIONS refer to milepost numbers — M.90.88 — the white highway mileposts along each highway. The access information also describes any facilities along that ride and any fees involved. Each ride has a corresponding map showing route, options and topography. The top of each map represents north, unless an arrow indicates otherwise.

The Ride Notes describe the details of each outing, giving you enough information to keep from getting lost. If you do become lost, backtrack until you know where you are. For a handy list of the easiest rides, those with the least vehicle traffic, single track, or the most challenging rides, see page 7.

All rides described in this book are open as we go to press. Unforeseen circumstances may close rides or portions of rides at any time. Please respect trail closures and private property. At Bored Feet we want your feedback. When rides are closed or someone says you can't ride there, other than seasonal closures and temporary closures due to logging, let us know. Our phone number and address are on the copyright page.

Whenever You Ride: About Safety

Whenever you ride your bike, you must assume responsibility for your own safety. Ride descriptions in this book point out hazards encountered when I rode the ride, but conditions change frequently. When you ride, be cautious, keep your senses focused on the ride, heed the book's warnings and assume that changes have occurred. Check on local conditions before you ride.

While many of these rides are described as having little or no vehicle traffic, always keep your senses honed. Bicycles and hikers are nearly silent, so you constantly need to look ahead, especially on narrow trails and blind corners. Use your ears to listen for the clip-clop of horses and the high whine of motor bikes. I once paused on the outside of a blind corner to await the passing of a motor bike. When the rider saw me he went into a skid and nearly plowed into me before gaining control. Pull off on the inside of corners, giving plenty of room.

Rider's Responsibilities

These rules of conduct, developed by the International Mountain Bicycling Association and National Off-Road Bicycle Association, are just good common sense. Heed them!

1. YIELD RIGHT OF WAY TO OTHER TRAVELERS. Slow to walking speed or stop, especially on narrow trails. When riding roads open to motor vehicles, obey all traffic regulations.

2. USE CAUTION WHEN PASSING FROM BEHIND. Make your presence known well in advance.

3. CONTROL YOUR BIKE. Excessive speed causes injuries and threat

11

ens other trail users.

4. RIDE OPEN TRAILS ONLY. Respect closures, and don't trespass on private property.

5. PRACTICE MINIMUM IMPACT CYCLING. Don't ride soft soils shortly after rain. When you come to a muddy section of track, walk your bike until you're again on firm tread. Don't create new trails.

6. DON'T DISTURB LIVESTOCK OR WILDLIFE. When passing equestrians, give horses a wide berth and make voice contact. Give all animals extra room and time to react to you.

7. DON'T LITTER. Perhaps you can haul out what someone else left.

8. ALWAYS WEAR A HELMET WHEN YOU RIDE.

9. BE PREPARED. Carry necessary supplies, including tire and chain repair kits, pump, water, snacks, basic first aid. Read up on the ride before you go. Be ready for weather changes.

When You Bike in Jackson State Forest

Nearly half the rides in this book explore this 50,000-acre working state forest between Fort Bragg, Mendocino and Willits. Jackson State Forest is managed jointly for timber harvest and recreation, so when logging is in progress in a particular area, that area will be closed to recreational users.

When planning a ride, it's best to call ahead to find out what areas are closed. The state forest office is open Monday through Friday from 8 to 5 (closed holidays) — (707)964-5674. If you cannot call ahead, as you approach the ride and when riding, look for signs indicating "Area closed for timber harvest." Some areas are posted "Area closed to motor vehicles," so don't confuse the two. It is extremely dangerous to be in an area when logging is in progress.

Keep in mind that ride descriptions may not be accurate after an area has been logged. New roads may have been built, old roads closed, or intersections and the general landscape changed drastically. When this is the case, use extra caution, checking maps and descriptions more frequently.

Be aware that the state forest is open to hunting, unlike state parks and areas adjacent to public thoroughfares. It is best to avoid riding in the state forest during hunting season, especially deer season from mid-August through September, also a good time to avoid Sherwood Road and other remote back roads.

Maps for rides in the state forest are adapted from the official state forest map, May 1995 edition. Jackson State Forest occasionally revises the map. To get a copy of the most recent state forest map, send $6.24 to Jackson State Forest, 802 N. Main St., Fort Bragg, CA 95437.

Riding Tips: To help you ride more efficiently

STRETCH. Doing a couple of minutes stretching before and after you ride will help you avoid injury and use your bike more efficiently.

RELAX. Tense riders crash more. Focus on feeling the machine and the placement of your weight on it, not on thinking about what you should be doing.

BIKE AS PART OF YOUR BODY. Think of your bike as an extension of your body. Minor changes in your body position on the machine have major effects on maneuverability. Find some gentle terrain and experiment with shifting body weight forward on ascents, back for downhills, keeping a low center of gravity, and turning your shoulders to initiate turns. Balance is a key to efficient riding.

SHIFT THOSE GEARS. Assertive gear shifting is one key to maximizing your machine's potential. As you ride, anticipate the gear shifts you'll make in the terrain immediately ahead, striving for smooth transitions. If you're pedaling rapidly, try a higher gear. When you're really straining at slow revolutions, it's time for a lower gear — if you have one.

OBSTACLES. Visualize a clear path around any obstacles. If you focus on the obstacle, even on not hitting it, a mental magnet often seems to steer you into the obstruction.

HILL CLIMBING. Start in a low gear, even the lowest gear for steeper ascents. Spread body weight forward along the bike, leaning into the incline while keeping enough weight back on your seat to avoid unweighting the rear wheel.

DESCENTS. Before long descents, lower your bike seat a couple of inches. A lower center of gravity gives more control. The steeper the hill, the farther back you want your weight, thighs gripping the seat, brakes in hand. Use front and rear brakes together, keeping in mind that each wheel's braking power is proportionate to the weight on the wheel at that moment. Keep pedals parallel to ground, with front pedal slightly higher.

CORNERING. Focus your weight on the pedals rather than the seat, allowing quicker shifting of body weight. Point your shoulders into the turn. Push the outside pedal down and put more weight on it, keeping your weight centered on the bike. Keep knees bent, ready to absorb changes in terrain. Avoid oversteering.

RIDING THROUGH SAND. Keep your momentum going into the sand. Sit back enough to let the front wheel float, then pedal evenly, trying to maintain momentum. If the bike skids, lightly steer with the direction the bike takes. Don't oversteer or steer against it, or you'll likely spill.

CLEAN AND GREASED. Keep your bike clean and lubricated between rides. Not only will it last longer, it'll work more efficiently.

So let's ride!

Ride #1

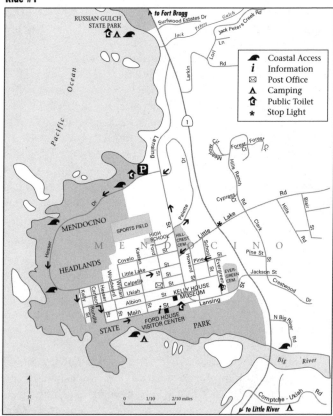

1

Mendocino Headlands State Park

Heeser Drive, Little Lake Street & Lansing Street with options on other town streets

The seaside grandeur of the Mendocino Headlands provides a dramatic back-drop to this short and easy ramble suitable for families. Whether you've seen the convoluted headlands in movies, on television or in person only once or a thousand times, experiencing them from a bike with the salty breeze in your face is an exhilarating experience. The headlands proffer a multitude of moods: sun-sparkled and becalmed, fog-shrouded, windswept with surf churning, verdant and speckled with wildflowers, or autumn's golden grasses at dawn, midday or glorious sunset. From this ride at the right time of year you may see whales spouting offshore, kites dancing, or hear a symphony playing, but whenever you visit, don't stay away on the flimsy excuse that you've been there before or that everyone does it.

DIRECTIONS TO STARTING POINT: Turn west off Highway One at the traffic signal onto Little Lake Road (M.50.85). At the stop sign, turn right on Lansing Street and go .3 mile. Turn left on Heeser Drive and go .2 mile to parking lot and restrooms on the right. (You can also start this loop from virtually anywhere in the village of Mendocino.)

WARNING!: Please stay on pavement or gravel parking lot. An experienced cyclist was killed in 1995 after he left the pavement for a narrow dirt bluff-edge trail — his pedal hit an embankment and pitched him fifty feet down into the churning surf. Bluff-edge trails are extremely unsafe for cyclists and subject to severe erosion from knobby tires.

ELEVATION AT START: 70 feet

OPTION 1:   Heeser Drive, Little Lake Street, Lansing Street.
Easy, 1.8-mile loop, medium vehicle traffic.
Elevation Gain/Loss: 120 feet+/120 feet-

OPTION 2: Heeser Drive, Kelly Street, Ukiah Street, Heeser Street, Main Street to Presbyterian Church and return.
Easy, 3 miles round trip, medium vehicle traffic.
Elevation Gain/Loss: 80 feet+/80 feet-

OPTION 3: Follow Option 2 to church, loop back on Evergreen Street, Pine Street, Howard Street, Little Lake Road, Lansing Street, Palette Drive, Lansing Street.
Easy, 2.9-mile loop, medium vehicle traffic.
Elevation Gain/Loss: 150 feet+/150 feet-

OPTION 4: Add Ride #2, 3, 4 or 6 to any of above. Rides #2 and 3 start 2 miles north (1.4 miles on Highway One). Ride #4 starts .5 mile south (on Highway One) of Presbyterian Church. Ride #6 is up Little Lake Road.

SURFACE: Paved roads and streets

FACILITIES: Restrooms, water, picnic tables at start and around Ford House Visitor Center, commercial facilities in town.

Ride Notes

Descend west on Heeser Drive, which soon turns south and contours beside convoluted ocean bluffs. If you want a closer look at the rugged shore and churning surf, detour to the right at .6 mile into the south-west parking lot, which extends onto a dramatic promontory surrounded on three sides by ocean, with a natural bridge on the right.

Heeser Drive turns east after the southwest lot. Option 1 follows that road, which climbs a short hill, becoming Little Lake Street as it passes the Mendocino Art Center. After a stop sign at 1 mile, continue straight to the next stop sign, at Lansing Street. Turn left, climb over a hill and descend to 1.6 miles, where you turn left on Heeser Drive, returning to your starting point at 1.8 miles.

OPTION 2: For a longer ride, follow Option 1 to .8 mile, then turn right on Kelly Street and go two short blocks. As you pass a house with unusual abalone folk art on your right, turn left on Ukiah Street, pedal up one block, then turn right to descend Heeser Street. It soon ends at the west end of Main Street. Turn left and ascend Main Street, passing the Ford House Visitor Center and Museum on your right at 1.3 miles (picnic tables, restrooms, water), then continuing to the Presbyterian Church (established 1868) at 1.5 miles. Today the back of the building faces Main Street because the original coast road passed on the other side of the stately building — go take a look. Option 2 concludes by retracing your route down Main Street and around the headlands to your starting point, 3 miles round trip.

OPTION 3: Follow Option 2 to the Presbyterian Church at 1.5 miles, then continue up Main Street to the next corner, where you turn left and ascend Evergreen Street two blocks to its end. Turn left and contour along Pine Street until it ends, then go right a block on Howard Street. Go left on Little Lake to the stop sign, then right up Lansing Street to the top of the hill. Turn right there onto Palette Drive, which loops around the Hill House and through a residential neighborhood with some grand ocean views. Descend to the end of Palette Drive at 2.6 miles, go right on Lansing Street briefly, then turn left on Heeser Drive and descend to your starting point at 2.9 miles.

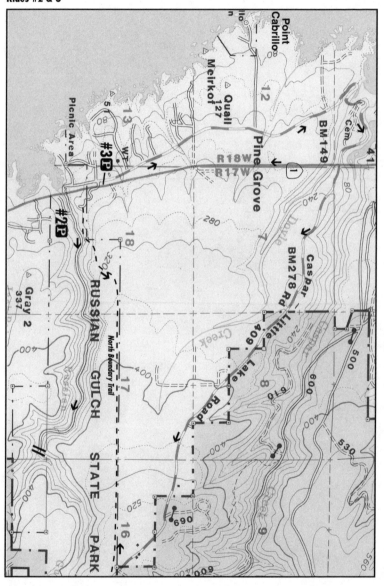

Russian Gulch Canyon & Headlands

Russian Gulch State Park roads, with option on North Boundary Trail

This easy ride explores the verdant canyon of Russian Gulch. The paved track ascends gently, flirting with the small creek's lazy lower end as it meanders through the park campground, then hugging its banks beside small cascades, winding through the deep slot carved by the dancing waters. The bike path ends at a shaded cul-de-sac where picnic tables invite you to linger. A handy bike rack encourages you to park and lock your wheels, then saunter ¾ mile up the narrow path to a lovely waterfall.

Your ride back down canyon is over so quickly, you'll be tempted to explore two short spur roads to the magical beach beneath the highway bridge and the flower-studded high headlands. For a moderate ride, add Option 5.

DIRECTIONS TO STARTING POINT: Turn west off Highway One north of Mendocino at Point Cabrillo Drive (M.52.95), then immediately turn left to park entrance. Go downhill .4 mile to the year-round parking beside the clubhouse.

ELEVATION AT START: 20 feet

OPTION 1: Russian Gulch Canyon.
Easy, 4.4 miles round trip, little or no vehicle traffic.
Elevation Gain/Loss: 100 feet+/100 feet-

OPTION 2: Add spur to Russian Gulch Beach.
Easy, add .4 mile round trip, light vehicle traffic.
Elevation Gain/Loss: minimal

OPTION 3: Add spur to headlands overlook.
Easy, add 1.2 miles round trip, light vehicle traffic.
Elevation Gain/Loss: Add 120 feet+/120 feet-

OPTION 4: Add Point Cabrillo Drive (see Ride #3).
Easy, add 6.1 miles, light to medium vehicle traffic.
Elevation Gain/Loss: Add 500 feet+/500 feet-

OPTION 5: Add North Boundary Trail.

> Moderate, add 7 miles round trip, single and double track.
> Elevation Gain/Loss: Add 720 feet+/720 feet-

SURFACE: Paved, except Option 5

FEE: $5/vehicle day use/parking. No charge to bike in from elsewhere.

FACILITIES: Picnic area, water, restrooms, phone, campground open April–Oct.

Ride Notes

Ride east on the campground road, with Russian Gulch Creek on your right. Leave the campground by .4 mile and pass another parking area, then a gate blocking motorized traffic. The paved trail continues up canyon on a slight incline, winding beside the stream. Pass a weeping wall on your left before 1 mile. Ascend gradually as the creek picks up speed. Wrap left around a tall mossy rock at 1.4 miles, then climb moderately past murmuring cascades. Ascend gently through forest to the bike path's end at 2.2 miles, where picnic tables beneath redwoods invite a snack. You might lock your bike and walk ¾ mile up to a delightful waterfall. Ride down canyon to the starting point at 4.4 miles.

OPTION 2 goes left on the road just west of the parking area, following it .4 mile to the beach at Russian Gulch Cove. When you've had enough of this dramatic spot, return to the starting point.

OPTION 3: Game for more? The big hill climbing toward the park entrance looks more imposing than it is. Ride up it, gaining 100 feet by .3 mile. Turn left on the paved spur road signed "Picnic Area" and follow it west to its end at .6 mile for grand views of the park's headlands, and if it's not too foggy, Mendocino Headlands a mile south. A footpath heads west to Devil's Punchbowl. Ride back to the junction at .8 mile, where a picnic area on the right offers a superb spot with wonderful views. Return to starting point or ride Option 4 or 5.

OPTION 4: Beyond the picnic area, instead of turning right on the main park road, turn left and ascend past the entrance kiosk, then take Point Cabrillo Drive. See Ride #3 for a full description.

OPTION 5: For a more challenging ride, pass the kiosk and go right. Cautiously cross Highway One to follow the paved road past headquarters. In .3 mile from the highway, go left and ascend the signed North Boundary Trail, a fun dirt track of 3 miles. See Ride #6, Option 3 for details.

3

Point Cabrillo to Caspar Beach

Point Cabrillo Drive, with options in Caspar South Subdivision, on Highway One, Road 409 & North Boundary Trail

This pleasant ocean view ride follows a length of old Highway One through Pine Grove, site of a pioneer settlement, past Point Cabrillo, then down to tiny Caspar State Beach. The road then climbs past the site of the Caspar Lumber Company mill to return to Highway One. At the highway, the first option returns the way you came, with the choice of a short loop through the Caspar South Subdivision. Option 2 returns along a busy stretch of Highway One. For a more challenging ride, Option 3 climbs east on paved Road 409 (Caspar-Little Lake Road), then follows the North Boundary Trail (a narrow double track with some single track) of Russian Gulch State Park for a fun descent through varied terrain, returning you to Highway One just across the busy highway from your starting point. The last option explores the heart of nearby Russian Gulch State Park, described in Ride #2.

DIRECTIONS TO STARTING POINT: Turn west off Highway One, north of Mendocino, at M.52.95 onto Point Cabrillo Drive. Turn right and park on the broad shoulder.

ELEVATION AT START: 170 feet

OPTION 1: Point Cabrillo Drive north and return.
Easy, 6.1 or 6.9 miles round trip, light vehicle traffic.
Elevation Gain/Loss: 500 feet+/500 feet-

OPTION 2: Point Cabrillo Drive, Highway One.
Easy, 4.8-mile loop, heavy traffic on highway.
Elevation Gain/Loss: 350 feet+/350 feet-

OPTION 3: Point Cabrillo Drive, Road 409, North Boundary Trail.
Moderate, 9.5-mile loop, light to medium vehicle traffic.
Elevation Gain/Loss: 720 feet+/720 feet-

OPTION 4: Add Russian Gulch (see Ride #2).

Easy, up to 6 miles round trip, light vehicle traffic.

SURFACE: Paved (except Option 3, final leg)

FACILITIES: Small convenience store and full service private campground at Caspar Beach RV Park (964-3306).

MAP: Page 18

Ride Notes

Follow Point Cabrillo Drive north, watching for traffic. The two-lane road follows the contours of the land, dipping gently through numerous small gullies, then climbing back to the bench of the second terrace. At 1.2 miles you pass the paved access road to Point Cabrillo Headlands Preserve. Its 300 acres are off limits to bikes, but offer an easy walk to the 1909 lighthouse surrounded by magnificent headlands. European settlement here started in the 1850s, when the farming community called Pine Grove prospered. Native American settlement in the area has been traced back 10,000 years.

Continue north on Point Cabrillo Drive. After a couple more dips and rises, at 1.7 miles you start the descent to Caspar Beach. At 1.8 and 2.1 miles, the two ends of South Caspar Drive offer a loop of about a mile. At the second side road, slow down for the winding descent to the beach at 2.3 miles. A small convenience store is on the right.

Point Cabrillo Drive soon turns away from the Pacific Ocean and ascends east along Caspar Creek, overlooking the site of a large sawmill that was torn down in 1956. Climb moderately past a spur to an old cemetery on the right, winding up to Highway One at 3 miles. Option 1 turns back, retracing your route for a 6.1-mile round trip. Extend your outing with a loop through Caspar South Subdivision (add .8 mile), a walk to the Point Cabrillo Lighthouse and Preserve, or one of the other options.

OPTION 2: If you are game for highway traffic, from the north end of Point Cabrillo Drive, turn right and ride the shoulder south, climbing gradually to the top of the hill at 3.9 miles, then descending to Point Cabrillo Drive at 4.8 miles. Turn right twice to return to your starting point.

OPTION 3: For a more challenging ride, from the north end of Point Cabrillo Drive, cautiously cross the highway and pedal east up Caspar-

Little Lake Road (Road 409). Ascend moderately to 4 miles, then gradually following a ridge.

At 6.4 miles, just after your road becomes dirt, turn right onto a dirt track signed "Horse Camp." Go .1 mile, then take the double track behind the brown gate marked "No parking." This is the North Boundary Trail, which soon turns to single track as it dips and rises through a rough section with a sand trap at the bottom. The trail alternately contours and descends, double track in some places, single track in others, mostly smooth tread but with a few rough sections disrupted by the big roots of trees along the path.

At 8.7 miles the track veers left to follow a power line, then leaves the wires to descend through forest. (For more about the North Boundary Trail, see Ride #6.) Where the track ends at 9.1 miles, turn right onto pavement and ride through the state parks maintenance yard and past park headquarters. At 9.4 miles you cross Highway One and turn right, immediately coming to your starting point.

OPTION 4: Since you're already parked just outside Russian Gulch State Park, it costs nothing to ride south into the heart of the park, where you can add up to 6 miles of mostly easy track. It's .4 mile to the start of Ride #2.

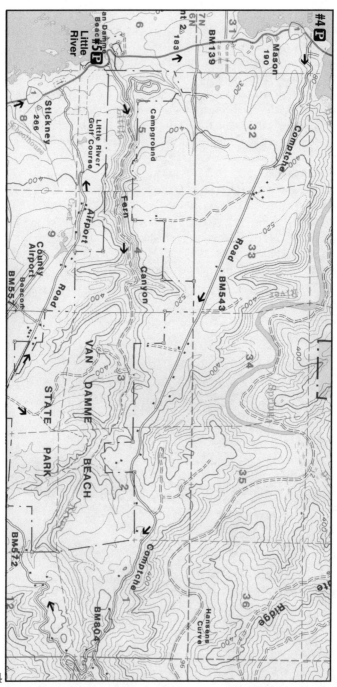

4

Comptche Road/Little River Loop

Comptche-Ukiah Road, with options on Little River-Airport Road, Albion-Little River Road, Highway One & Van Damme State Park trails

This classic road ride explores back roads southeast of Mendocino, hilly wooded country that feeds three coastal rivers. Once you reach the 820-foot summit at 5.6 miles, you can return the way you came or choose from three loops that include 2 to 6 miles on Highway One. You can also ride 15 miles to Comptche — or all the way to Ukiah for a 45-mile (one way) marathon back road experience.

DIRECTIONS TO STARTING POINT: Turn west off Highway One south of Mendocino (M.50.00) onto frontage road and park. Cautiously cross Highway One and head east on Comptche-Ukiah Road. If you rent a bike from Catch-a-Canoe & Bicycles Too, east of the highway, you can park there.

ELEVATION AT START: 60 feet

OPTION 1: Up Comptche-Ukiah Road and return.
Moderate, 11.8 miles round trip (or strenuous 29.4 miles round trip) light to medium vehicle traffic.
Elevation Gain/Loss: 1060 feet+/1060 feet-

OPTION 2: Up Comptche-Ukiah Road, down Little River-Airport Road to Pygmy Forest, descend through Van Damme State Park, north on Highway One.
Moderate, 15.8-mile loop, light to medium vehicle traffic, except Highway One — heavy vehicle traffic.
Elevation Gain/Loss: 1240 feet+/1240 feet-

OPTION 3: Up Comptche-Ukiah Road, down Little River-Airport Road, north on Highway One.
Moderate, 14.4-mile loop, light to medium vehicle traffic, except Highway One — heavy vehicle traffic.
Elevation Gain/Loss: 1190 feet+/1190 feet-

OPTION 4: Up Comptche-Ukiah Road, down Little River-Airport Road, down Albion-Little River Road, north on Highway One.

Moderate, 18.3-mile loop, light to medium vehicle traffic, except Highway One — heavy vehicle traffic.

Elevation Gain/Loss: 1610 feet+/1610 feet-

SURFACE: Paved (Option 2 has 2 miles of dirt track)

FACILITIES: Mendocino's only bike shop near the start of this ride, restrooms at Van Damme State Park on Highway One, small markets at Little River and Comptche.

Ride Notes

From Highway One, ascend east on Comptche-Ukiah Road. You must stay on the road's shoulder, especially on the winding first mile, easily the most hazardous part of Option 1. Ascend steeply from .2 mile on winding two-lane blacktop beneath tall forest. Your ascent turns moderate before 1 mile, rounding one more curve at 1.3 miles to begin a long straightaway.

By 1.6 miles your hill turns gradual as the road crosses the Mendocino White Plains, home of the dwarfed trees known as pygmy forest. At 2.6 miles a short footpath (no bikes please) on the right explores this bizarre habitat.

Comptche-Ukiah Road tops the first hill at 3 miles, dips and rises to a second top before the end of the straightaway at 3.5 miles, then descends slightly through gentle curves as the pavement narrows. Resume a gradual ascent by 4 miles. The hill turns moderate by 4.6 miles, with views left over the canyons of Big River. The winding road reaches a summit of 820 feet at 5.6 miles, then descends slightly to Little River-Airport Road, on your right at 5.9 miles. The easiest ride turns back here, an 11.8-mile round trip. (For a longer, strenuous version of Option 1, continue on Comptche-Ukiah Road 8.8 miles to the hamlet of Comptche in an inland valley. The trip out has two sustained descents bracketed by short climbs, so the trip back involves an arduous ascent. Total distance is 29.4 miles round trip, total elevation change: 2970 feet+ /2970 feet-.)

OPTIONS 2, 3 & 4: Turn right on Little River-Airport Road, a narrow, paved two lane, and ascend briefly past the old Ellison Schoolhouse. Descend from 6 miles, then contour through forest along the flank of 1030-foot Mathison Peak. By 6.6 miles your winding road descends fitfully, with views over the wooded ridges and deep canyons of the Albion River on your left.

Around 7.8 miles, begin a long contour broken by two short ascents, passing through pockets of pygmy forest. After a straightaway, approach the Little River Y at 9.1 miles, where the options head different directions.

OPTION 2: Turn right at 9.1 miles into Van Damme State Park's Pygmy Forest parking area. At 9.2 miles a boardwalk on the right (pedestrians and wheelchair riders only) explores an extreme example of midget woods. Continue straight to a junction, then go left on the fire road, descending gradually, then moderately into Fern Canyon and the heart of the park. At 10.7 miles you must ford the Little River (easy in summer and autumn, may be deep in winter) to reach the end of the Fern Canyon Trail 150 feet beyond. Follow the track downstream past remote campsites, soon coming to pavement. After several bridged crossings of the stream in its deep fern-laden canyon, the track ends at 13.2 miles. Follow the park road out to Highway One at 13.9 miles. Turn right and ride the highway shoulder toward Mendocino, returning to your starting point at 15.8 miles.

OPTION 3: This choice continues down Little River-Airport Road, contouring past the Y junction, then along a straightaway beside the Mendocino County Airport. Begin a gradual descent by 10 miles. The downhill turns moderate beneath tall forest by 10.7 miles. After the upper end of Little River Golf Course at 11.6 miles, sit back for a steepening descent. Be certain you stop before your road ends at Highway One at 12 miles. Otherwise you may be buried in the historic Little River Cemetery across the highway!

Turn right and cautiously ride the shoulder of Highway One as it descends through the tiny town of Little River, passing a market and inns at 12.2 miles, then winding down to the mouth of the Little River at 12.5 miles. The beach parking lot on the left offers a good spot for a break, with pit toilets, picnic tables and beach access.

To finish the loop, return to Highway One for the winding moderate ascent north. The Shoreline Highway soon straightens out, topping the hill by 13.2 miles, then dips and rises twice before a short drop back to your starting point at 14.4 miles. For a less trafficked finish, you can turn left at 13.8 miles onto Brewery Gulch Road, an old stretch of highway that hugs the shore of Mendocino Bay for a scenic finish of roughly the same length.

OPTION 4: Back at the Little River Y at 9.1 miles, turn left on Albion-Little River Road, which contours past the end of the airport runway, then passes through pygmy forest. Start a slight descent around 10 miles, as tall forest replaces the dwarf trees. Ascend over a couple of small rises before 10.6 miles, then start a long winding downhill. Most of the drop is moderate, with views on the left down to the nearby Albion River. By 12.2 miles the Pacific Ocean appears ahead as the descent ends. The road ends at 12.4 miles, coming to Highway One.

Turn right and ride the highway shoulder north, dipping past Albion River Inn and rising over Albion Head, then descending through Dark Gulch at 13.4 miles. Ascend gradually to the Heritage House, then moderately through sharp curves. From 14.2 miles, contour through more curves, then start a moderate descent at 14.8 miles. Drop to only 30 feet above sea level at Buckhorn Gulch at 15.3 miles, then climb before dropping to Little River-Airport Road at 15.9 miles. Follow the description at the end of Option 3 for the final 2.4 miles to complete an 18.3-mile loop.

5

Fern Canyon to Pygmy Forest

Van Damme State Park roads and trails, with options on Little River-Airport Road, Albion-Little River Road & Highway One

Little River's popular Fern Canyon Trail was once a skid trail used by oxen teams to haul immense cut redwoods down to the mill, located where the park visitor center is today. The sawmill has been gone for a century now, and the lush canyon shows few scars of its logging days. Today you'll follow a paved track along a stream in a deep canyon draped with ten kinds of ferns. Even the redwoods have returned. Where the gentle ride ends, a more challenging dirt track climbs to the curious Pygmy Forest on the plateau above. From there you can return the way you came for a nearly traffic-free ride, or loop back on paved roads, including .5 mile on Highway One.

DIRECTIONS TO STARTING POINT: Van Damme State Park is on Highway One at Little River (M.48.05) south of Mendocino. You can park in the beach parking lot west of the highway (no fee), or turn east and enter the park (fee). This description starts at the beach lot.

WARNING!: Go slow and watch for walkers and joggers on this popular trail.

ELEVATION AT START: 20 feet

OPTION 1: Fern Canyon Trail from Highway One to end.
Easy, 6.4 miles round trip, little or no vehicle traffic.
Elevation Gain/Loss: 220 feet+/220 feet-

OPTION 2: Fern Canyon Trail, up fire road to Pygmy Forest & return.
Moderate, 9.2 miles round trip, little or no vehicle traffic.
Elevation Gain/Loss: 650 feet+/650 feet-

OPTION 3: Fern Canyon Trail to Pygmy Forest, return by Little River-Airport Road and Highway One.
Moderate, 8.1-mile loop, little or no vehicle traffic on first leg, medium to heavy traffic on last leg.
Elevation Gain/Loss: 610 feet+/610 feet-

OPTION 4: Fern Canyon Trail to Pygmy Forest, return by Albion-Little River Road and Highway One.

Moderate, 12-mile loop, little or no vehicle traffic on first leg, medium to heavy traffic on last leg.

Elevation Gain/Loss: 1030 feet+/1030 feet-

SURFACE: Mixed paved park roads and dirt trails, Options 3 and 4 have short and medium highway mileage.

FEE: $5/vehicle day use/parking to drive into the park (east of Highway One).

FACILITIES: Picnic tables, restrooms, phone, campground (open year round), environmental camps 2.5 miles along the route.

MAP: Page 24

Ride Notes

From the beach parking lot, cautiously cross Highway One and head east into the park, passing the entrance kiosk, then a picnic area on the right at .1 mile. As the road forks at .2 mile, stay to the right, riding through the campground, site of the Little River sawmill and mill pond. Your level road passes restrooms and crosses two sturdy bridges over the Little River. Pass the end of the campground and come to the parking area for the Fern Canyon Trail at .7 mile. (You can start from here if you pay the $5 day-use fee.)

The pavement, often coated with redwood duff, narrows to double track as it heads up canyon. Canyon walls lushly draped with ferns and other moisture-loving plants rise steeply on both sides. Your track ascends slightly to 1.2 miles, following close beside the stream. Descend slightly past a flood-ravaged break in the pavement, then cross the first of the new bicycle/pedestrian bridges across the diminutive river, followed promptly by the second bridge before 1.5 miles.

Continue up the canyon on the winding track, quickly crossing two more bridges. Begin a steady gradual ascent, crossing three more bridges before 2 miles. Pass the first of ten environmental (walk- or bike-in) camps around 2.5 miles. The campsites, spread out over the next .2 mile, offer a great place to escape from it all.

Pass a deep side canyon on the right, then one on the left by 2.7 miles. Fern Canyon broadens as you wind sharply right and left, contouring along the river. By 2.8 miles the track forks into a small loop. Whichever fork you take, the road ends before 3.2 miles. Option 1 retraces your route downstream.

OPTION 2: For a more strenuous workout, take the dirt double track that heads south from the east end of the paved loop, dropping to ford the river (may be deep in winter and spring), then ascending a side canyon. The climb starts gradually, but soon turns moderate as it switchbacks to the right to traverse the canyon wall on bumpy tread.

Switchback left at another side canyon at 3.5 miles and continue up better tread. By 3.8 miles your ascent eases as you gain a ridgetop and follow it to the coastal terrace above the canyon. At 4.4 miles you pass a junction with a footpath and contour through pygmy forest to the upper parking lot at 4.6 miles. Option 2 returns the way you came.

OPTIONS 3 & 4 both follow the pavement out to Little River-Airport Road at 4.7 miles. Turn right and promptly come to the intersection known as the Little River Y. Option 3 descends Little River-Airport Road on the right, dropping to Highway One at 7.6 miles, then going right along the highway for .5 mile to return to your starting point.

OPTION 4 goes left at the Y to descend Albion-Little River Road to Highway One at Albion, then follows the highway north to the starting point for a 12-mile loop. For more details about Options 3 and 4, see Ride #4, Options 3 and 4.

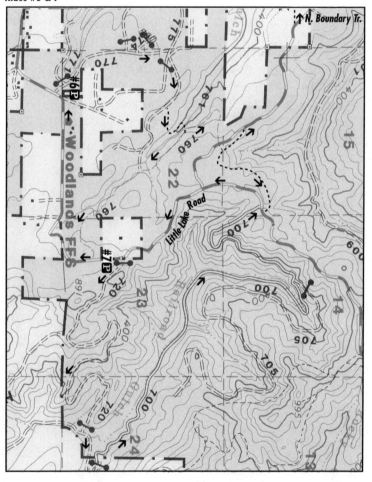

32

6

Headwaters of Russian Gulch

Jackson State Forest Road 770, Little Lake-Sherwood Trail, Road 760 & Little Lake Road, with options on North Boundary Trail, Road 409 & Highway One

This ride offers many choices of starting point and options along the way. While our description starts east of town where Road 770 leaves Little Lake Road, this loop's proximity to the town of Mendocino allows you to start in town. There is even a dedicated bike lane for the first mile up Little Lake Road. The loop itself offers a variety of terrain and tread, from broad, level gravel road, to easy single track to more challenging single track, with Option 3 following paved Highway One for 2 miles.

DIRECTIONS TO STARTING POINT: Turn east off Highway One at the stoplight on Little Lake Road (M.50.85). Go 3 miles to where Road 770, also known as Powers Road, takes off on your left (M.3.1). Park on Road 770.

ELEVATION AT START: 600 feet

OPTION 1: Road 770, Little Lake-Sherwood Trail, Road 760, Little Lake Road. Easy, 4.3 mile-loop, light to medium vehicle traffic. Elevation Gain/Loss: 360 feet+/360 feet-

OPTION 2: Road 770, Little Lake-Sherwood Trail, Little Lake Road. Easy, 5.7 mile-loop, light to medium vehicle traffic. Elevation Gain/Loss: 400 feet+/400 feet-

OPTION 3: Road 770, Little Lake-Sherwood Trail, Road 409, North Boundary Trail, Highway One, Little Lake Road. Moderate, 11.5-mile loop, light to medium vehicle traffic except on Highway One — heavy traffic. Elevation Gain/Loss: 890 feet+/890 feet-

OPTION 4: Add Ride #7. Moderate, add 7.7-mile loop, light to medium vehicle traffic. Elevation Gain/Loss: Add 780 feet+/780 feet-

SURFACE: Mixed double and single track and pavement

FACILITIES: At the Mendocino Area State Parks Headquarters (Option 3) you'll find a picnic table and restrooms.

Ride Notes

Head north on broad, level Road 770. After .1 mile you merge with the Little Lake-Sherwood Trail, .5 mile from its start. Road 770 dips through a gully, the headwaters of South Fork Russian Gulch Creek, then contours through pygmy forest. Cross Road 775 at a right angle and continue on Road 770. After dipping through another small gully, turn left at 1.3 miles onto a narrow single track and make a gradual winding descent. Before 1.5 miles the descent turns steep and rutted — you'll probably want to walk this nasty stretch, only 300 feet long. You can soon remount your bike to finish the descent, but you'll want to get off again at 1.6 miles to cross the deeply eroded gully, the main stem of Russian Gulch Creek. Veer right on the obvious track beyond the crossing, then come to unmarked Road 760 at 1.7 miles.

OPTION 1 turns right and follows Road 760 southeast to meet Little Lake Road in 1.3 miles. Head south-southeast alongside Russian Gulch Creek on the gentle incline of Road 760. It's a broad grassy track, but so overgrown in spots as to become single track. Descend briefly at 2 miles, coming to a crossing of a side stream where the bridge has been removed. About 50 feet before the chasm, a steep single track drops to creek side. Walk your bike down the treacherous hill, fork left to cross the side stream, then push very steeply up the other side to continue on Road 760. Ascend gradually on improving but uneven tread. By 2.4 miles you climb along a pretty section of creek where redwoods grow tall. The ascent turns moderate briefly, coming to a top at 2.7 miles. Drop across a tank trap and ascend to Little Lake Road at 3 miles, just south of Road 720 (see Ride #7). Veer right around a barrier to reach the pavement. Turn right and ascend briefly, then descend along Little Lake Road, returning to your starting point at 4.3 miles.

OPTIONS 2 & 3: Turn left on Road 760 to ascend moderately on uneven tread up a long hill, coming to very broad, graveled Road 409 (Caspar-Little Lake Road) at 2.25 miles.

The easiest ride would go right (Option 2) or left (Option 3) on Road 409. Our description takes the fun, easy single track trail across the road. When you come to the T intersection, Option 2 turns right while Option 3 turns left. The right turn follows Little Lake-Sherwood Trail as it contours east. When the track splits around 2.5 miles, go left (hiker/horse symbol on stump) and descend slightly heading north. At a junction before 2.9 miles, turn right and head east. Descend to a broad clearing at 3 miles, then ascend briefly to dirt Little Lake Road, 100 feet east of the Road 700 intersection. For a longer ride you can link with Rides #7 and 8 here. Otherwise turn right and follow paved Little Lake Road as it descends, with one short uphill, back to the start of Road 770 at 5.7 miles.

OPTION 3: Turn left and follow the single track on a gradual descent, returning to Road 409 at 2.9 miles. Go right on 409 and descend the broad gravel road to 3.5 miles (just before road turns paved). Turn left on the narrow road marked "Horse Camp." In .1 mile take the North Boundary Trail along the northern edge of Russian Gulch State Park. It starts behind a brown gate indicating no parking. The double track turns to single track and dips and rises through a rough section with a sand trap at the bottom. Then contour and descend gradually on smooth tread. After more loose sand at 4.7 miles, join a broader track and contour past Doyle Creek Mountain on your right, better known as the Old Caspar Dump. The route narrows to descend gradually on good tread with a few hazardous roots. At 5.8 miles the track veers left to follow a power line, then leaves it to descend through forest.

Where the track ends at 6.2 miles, turn right onto pavement and pass through the state parks maintenance yard. A picnic table on your right offers a spot to take a break. Descend past parks headquarters and come to Highway One before 6.5 miles.

The rest of your ride is on street or highway, so hug the right shoulder. Cautiously cross the highway, go left and follow it south, crossing two narrow bridges. After the second bridge, at 7.9 miles, you can turn right on Lansing Street if you started from town or want to extend your ride. Otherwise continue on the highway to the traffic signal at 8.5 miles, where you go left and ascend 3 miles on Little Lake Road, returning to Road 770 after 11.5 miles.

7

Big Hill Road to Railroad Gulch

Jackson State Forest Roads 720 & 700, Little Lake Road

This easy loop offers just enough change in elevation to make it fun. It's a good warm-up ride if you want to go for a marathon day of biking, a fine ride by itself if you don't want to push too hard. You can link with part of the Little Lake-Sherwood Trail if you want more single track or dirt, or you can add an extended road ride with Roads 408 and 409 plus Pt. Cabrillo Drive.

DIRECTIONS TO STARTING POINT: Turn east off Highway One at M.50.85 onto Little Lake Road. Go 4.3 miles to unmarked Road 720, which climbs uphill on your right behind a yellow gate. The ride is described from here, but you can also start at the junction of Roads 408 and 700 1.2 miles further, or from the Lily's Beach area at the bottom of the loop. The latter option is excellent on a warm day when you want to combine a swim with your ride, or when part of the group wants to laze by the river while the others cover some miles.

WARNING!: Road 720 is open to vehicle traffic from about May to October. Use particular caution on that leg when the gate is open.

ELEVATION AT START: 640 feet

OPTION 1: Roads 720, 700, Little Lake Road.
Moderate, 7.7-mile loop, light vehicle traffic on Roads 700 & 720, medium traffic on Little Lake Road.
Elevation Gain/Loss: 780 feet+/780 feet-

OPTION 2: Add Ride #8.
Moderate, 12 miles round trip, light vehicle traffic.
Elevation Gain/Loss: Add 1220 feet+/1220 feet-

OPTION 3: Add Ride #6.
Moderate, 4.3- or 11.5-mile loop, light to heavy vehicle traffic.
Elevation Gain/Loss: Add 360 feet+/360 feet- for short ride, 890 feet+/890 feet- for long ride.

SURFACE: Mixed, paved and dirt double track

FACILITIES: None, but when the weather is warm, you can swim at beaches along Big River where Roads 772 and 700 meet.

MAP: Page 32

Ride Notes

Road 720, also known as Big Hill Road, ascends moderately east on smooth dirt double track as it leaves Little Lake Road. After climbing .3 mile, reach the loop's summit and descend gradually through the forest. At .8 mile your descent turns moderate, dropping around big bends. Around 1.5 miles the forest thins on your left, offering views over Railroad Gulch and the canyon of Big River.

The moderate, winding downhill continues to 2.5 miles, turning steep toward the end. Slow down as the tread turns rough — you'll quickly meet a yellow gate with a narrow track around it on the left.

The terrain levels beyond the gate as you approach Big River and its Little North Fork. At an intersection our route bears left, but you might want to explore the right fork which quickly draws near the river. The left fork contours to another intersection at 2.8 miles. Turn left again and quickly come to another junction. Each intersection increases the odds of seeing motor vehicle traffic, so keep your eyes and ears open.

The latter junction is clearly marked "Road 700 — Mendocino." Stay to the left, making a short steep ascent to pass the entrance to the Mendocino Woodlands, a private camp that leases its beautiful property from the state park system.

Stay left again on Road 700 as it descends briefly, then contours along Railroad Gulch through a forest of large redwoods with lush undergrowth. Enjoy this mostly level stretch along the canyon floor, which continues to 4.5 miles. Railroad Gulch once held a spur line of the Mendocino Lumber Company railroad.

Ascend gradually to 5 miles, then begin a steady moderate ascent up the gulch. The climb continues to 6.4 miles, where Road 700 meets Road 408 and ends.

Option 1 bears left to follow the paved portion of Little Lake Road 1.3 miles back to your starting point. If you want to extend your ride, you have several options. **OPTION 2** is the road on your right, described in Ride #8, part of the Little Lake-Sherwood Trail. **OPTION 3** takes an easier choice, going right for just 50 feet, then turning left on a single track trail (also part of LLS Trail, as described in Ride #6). In .8 mile the single track meets Road 409. There you can turn left and follow 409 to its end at Road 408. Or continue on a steeper portion of the LLS Trail for up to 3 miles. It ends at M.2.8 on Little Lake Road. If you want to bail out early on the latter choice, you can take Road 760 to come out on Little Lake Road .15 mile below the starting point (see Ride #6, Option 1).

OPTION 1: Assuming you choose to go left on Road 408, descend briefly, then climb gradually on the pavement. Top out at Road 409 at 6.6 miles. Then Road 408 descends moderately to 7.1 miles before climbing again to return to your starting point at 7.7 miles.

Ride #8

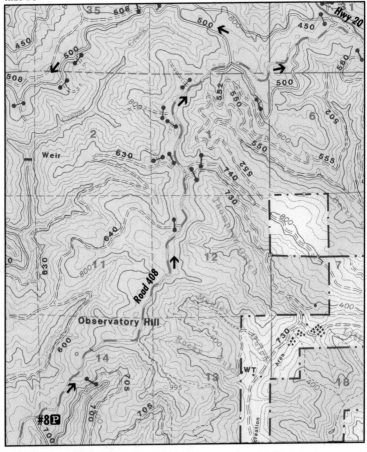

8

Little Lake Road Section of Little Lake-Sherwood Trail

Dirt portion of County Road 408, with options on other parts of Little Lake-Sherwood Trail, Road 500, Highway One & Road 409

This leg of the pioneer stagecoach route from Mendocino to Willits (once called Little Lake) remains much as it was in the nineteenth century, except that the ruts once made by metal-rimmed wooden wheels are now worn by rubber tires. You are likely to encounter more vehicle traffic than cyclists here, but traffic overall is usually light.

The narrow road follows a ridge line virtually for its entire length, offering some grand views of coast and ocean to the west and wooded hills in most every other direction. Links with other rides give you numerous choices for longer excursions.

DIRECTIONS TO STARTING POINT: Turn east off Highway One at M.50.85 onto Little Lake Road. Go 5.65 miles and park at the intersection of unpaved roads 408 and 700.

ELEVATION AT START: 630 feet

OPTION 1: Road 408 to Highway 20 and back.
Moderate, 12 miles round trip, light vehicle traffic.
Elevation Gain/Loss: 1220 feet+/1220 feet-

OPTION 2: Road 408, return by Road 500, Highway One & Road 409
Moderate, 18.4 mile-loop, light to medium vehicle traffic, except on Highway One — heavy traffic.
Elevation Gain/Loss: 1360 feet+/1360 feet-

OPTION 3: Add southern end of Little Lake-Sherwood Trail, see Ride #6.
Moderate, add 6 or 6.8 miles round trip, little or no vehicle traffic.
Elevation Gain/Loss: Add 830 feet+/830 feet-

OPTION 4: Continue north on Little Lake-Sherwood Trail from Highway 20. Strenuous, add up to 44.3 miles each way, light vehicle traffic. Elevation Gain/Loss: Add 1510 feet+/1830 feet- to 7.1 miles, 5900 feet+/5320 feet- to Willits (one way).

SURFACE: Dirt road

Ride Notes

The double track of this old stage road ascends briefly, then drops and contours. At .5 mile you veer right and begin a sustained steep ascent, the longest on Road 408. By 1.2 miles the hill turns gradual, then passes the Forest History Trail (see Rides #9 and 10). The ascent ends by 1.4 miles as you pass Observatory Hill.

Your road follows the ridgetop dividing the watersheds of Big River on your right and Caspar Creek on the left, providing a repeating down-up pattern. Descend slightly, ascend, then contour to 2.4 miles, followed by a short descent past Road 640 on the left (see Ride #11). Contour past Roads 730 and 740 on the right followed by Road 630 on the left at 3.2 miles. A short drop and rise lead into a large clearcut, then it's down and up again to 3.8 miles. A moderate downhill through forest ends back in the clearcut by 4 miles.

Stay left at the junction at 4.2 miles and go over and down a short steep hill. Drop to the junction with Road 500 at 4.4 miles. Option 1 continues north along the ridgetop on Road 408. (For an easier route, go right on 500, crossing 408 twice before Highway 20.) Option 2 goes left on Road 500, described below. Option 1 continues on Road 408, ascending moderately for .6 mile, with sections of rough tread cut by gullies offering a little technical challenge. At the top you get some roller coaster action as views open up to the east. Drop down to 5.4 miles, where Road 408 merges with Road 500. At 5.6 miles Road 408 is the unmarked right fork. (If you want to continue on the Little Lake-Sherwood Trail, see Option 4.) Road 408 descends to end at Highway 20 just short of 6 miles. Option 1 returns more or less the way you came.

OPTION 2: Back at the first junction of Roads 408 and 500, at 4.4 miles, go left and descend gradually on Road 500's broad, mostly smooth tread. Contour through pretty forest from 4.7 miles, coming to an immense clearcut by 5 miles. A slight descent passes Road 456 at 5.4 miles (see Ride #27). A long gradual ascent passes a massive stump hanging over the road, then returns to forest. Climb back into the clearcut by 6.7 miles, cresting a hill by 7.4 miles. Start a long descent, dropping gently through forest, passing Road 511 on your right at 7.8 miles (see Ride #19). Your downhill turns moderate by 8.4 miles, then eases before passing Road 520 at 9 miles (see Ride #12). The long downhill continues almost to Road 500's end at 12.4 miles. Turn left and descend to Highway One at 12.7 miles, then go left again.

Follow the highway across the Caspar Creek bridge to 13.2 miles, turn left on paved Road 409 and ascend moderately, then fitfully. At 16.3 miles (M.3.1), your ascent turns to dirt. Road 409 drops to its end at 18 miles. Turn left and go .4 mile to your starting point.

OPTION 3: An easier extension of Option 1 starts closer to Mendocino. Begin from Little Lake Road either at M.2.78, southern end of the Little Lake-Sherwood Trail, to add 3.4 miles (each way) of mixed single and double track; or at M.3.1, Road 770 (see Ride #6), to add 3 miles each way.

OPTION 4: The Little Lake-Sherwood Trail offers a 52-mile backwoods challenge from Mendocino to Willits on Highway 101. Option 1 explores only a small part of the lightly traveled trail, a route combining dirt and paved county roads, state forest roads, and short sections of single track. To continue north from Highway 20 on the LLS Trail, stay left at Option 1's 5.6-mile-point, descend Road 500 to its end, cross Highway 20 and find Road 90 slightly to the west. Descend Road 90 for .3 mile, then veer right and descend the eastern side of Camp One Loop. At the bottom end, turn right on Road 360 and follow it to Road 362. Turn left and ascend 362 to Jackass Pass. Take the single track descending northwest across private property — please stay on trail and go slow. In 3 miles from Jackass Pass, turn right on the dirt road that quickly crosses a bridge over the North Fork Noyo River. Turn right briefly, then go left and ascend Company Ranch Road for 1.5 miles. This brings you to Sherwood Road. A left turn would lead to Fort Bragg and Highway One in 5.5 miles. The LLS Trail turns right and ascends Sherwood Road. Ride #17 describes the 34 miles to Willits. Rides 22, 25 and 16 have details of specific sections.

9

Manly Gulch

Manly Gulch Trail, with options on Forest History Trail & Road 408

This single track offers one of the most exciting and challenging rides on the coast: twisting, narrow trail across steep, unforgiving terrain. This is not a place for beginners! While the name Manly might sound like a reference to macho criteria for making this ride, Manly Gulch really has a more feminine aspect: lush, curvaceous and deep. The ride back out of this steep canyon is an arduous, technically challenging ascent.

DIRECTIONS TO STARTING POINT: Turn east off Highway One at M.50.85 onto Little Lake Road. Go 6.8 miles (last mile is dirt) to M.6.95, start of the Forest History Trail, and park.

WARNING!: Go slow and watch for hikers, especially on the canyon's lower end.

ELEVATION AT START: 880 feet

OPTION 1: Forest History Trail to Manly Gulch Trail, Manly Gulch to bottom and return.
Advanced, 4.6 miles round trip, single track.
Elevation Gain/Loss: 770 feet+/770 feet-

OPTION 2: Add Forest History Trail, Ride #10.
Advanced, add 3 miles round trip, single track.
Elevation Gain/Loss: Add 760 feet+/760 feet-

OPTION 3: Add Little Lake Road, Ride #8.
Moderate, add 9.4 miles round trip to Highway 20, double track, light vehicle traffic.
Elevation Gain/Loss: Add 920 feet+/920 feet-

SURFACE: Dirt single track, except Option 3

MAP: Page 45

Ride Notes

Descend the winding, single-track Forest History Trail for .3 mile to a junction. Turn left on the single track signed "Camp 2 via Manly Gulch." (The Forest History Trail continues on the right, see Ride #10.) After a short moderate descent, Manly Gulch Trail contours across steep terrain from .4 to .7 mile. Around .5 mile, watch for a rustic, tire-eating wooden bridge — it may require a dismount. Soon after, your single track runs a gauntlet through a circle of redwoods, with only six inches to spare beyond the width of your handlebars.

By .8 mile you should know whether you are up for this challenging ride. It gets tougher, so turn back if you have doubts. Your single track descends vigorously, crossing another rickety bridge, then passing an old water tank. At 1.2 miles the track switchbacks sharply right, descending to a marked junction at 1.3 miles. Take the right fork, since the left fork has some very large gully crossings. Just 100 feet beyond the junction, the right fork crosses a small gully, then traverses a very steep slope where all riders should use caution and those with vertigo might choose to walk their bike or turn back.

The track descends to cross another gulch at 1.5 miles where you will need to dismount to cross. Descend to another gully crossing around 1.75 miles, where the two forks merge beyond the ford. Follow the track down the bottom of the gulch through lush vegetation. Though the riding gets easier overall, the gulch-bottom track offers a few surprises (perhaps even some traffic), so stay alert. Ford the stream twice, then cross a bridge made of iron railroad rails found on site. (The Mendocino Lumber Company Railroad navigated these gulches before any roads did.)

At 2.2 miles you cross a corduroy bridge to reach the left side of the gulch and stream. Continue downstream until your single track ends at a broader track where the canyon opens up. You have reached the boundary of the Mendocino Woodlands, a private camp. Your only choice is to turn back and ride back up to the ridge.

OPTION 2: If you want a longer ride when you get back to the ridge at 4.3 miles, instead of turning right to return to your starting point, go left and follow the Forest History Trail as described in Ride #10 to add 3 or more miles.

OPTION 3: From the starting point, you can ride north on Little Lake Road (Road 408) as described in Ride #8 from 1.3 miles, following the ridgetop up, down and around to Highway 20 in 4.7 miles.

10

Railroad Gulch East Slope

Forest History Trail, with option on Roads 705, 700 & 408

This challenging single track explores an attractive, wooded corner of the state forest in the Big River watershed. If you've never ridden single track before, don't start here. The steep terrain is too scary and unforgiving. But riders with single track experience will find this a fun descent, with a manageable return ascent. If you'd rather take a longer but easier way back, Option 3 describes a loop on Roads 705, 700 and 408 that has two hearty ascents, after a pleasant roller-coaster run. The truly fearless can add the even more challenging single track of Manly Gulch to the mix.

DIRECTIONS TO STARTING POINT: Same as Ride #9.

WARNING!: Go slow and watch for hikers.

ELEVATION AT START: 880 feet

OPTION 1: Forest History Trail to lower junction and return.
Advanced, 3.6 miles round trip.
Elevation Gain/Loss: 840 feet+/840 feet-

OPTION 2: Forest History Trail to 2.4 miles and return.
Advanced, 4.8 miles round trip.
Elevation Gain/Loss: 880 feet+/880 feet-

OPTION 3: Loop back on Roads 705, 700 and 408.
Moderate, 6.4-mile loop (with 1.4 miles single track), light vehicle traffic.
Elevation Gain/Loss: Add 770 feet+/770 feet-

OPTION 4: Add Manly Gulch, Ride #9.
Advanced, add 4 miles round trip.
Elevation Gain/Loss: Add 690 feet+/690 feet-

SURFACE: Dirt single track, except Option 3

Ride Notes

Descend the winding, single-track Forest History Trail for .3 mile to a junction with the Manly Gulch Trail (see Ride #9). Go straight, contouring, then ascending slightly to a second junction before .4 mile. The left fork is closed to cyclists — extremely steep across sensitive terrain, and the many wooden steps in the trail are hell on cyclists. Turn right on the Demonstration Forestry Section of the trail. Ascend gently on narrowing track across steep terrain, passing rocky sections of the mostly duff trail.

By .7 mile, begin a gradual descent that soon turns moderate on very narrow track across a steep slope. By 1.2 miles you can see Road 705 below. At 1.3 miles, leave the sidehill to contour and descend gradually along a ridgetop. A dip at 1.4 miles is where a vague path forks right to meet Road 705 (see Option 3). Climb briefly and resume descending. Pass a bogus spur at 1.6 miles that quickly leads out of the state forest.

Forest History Trail turns east, descending moderately but fitfully to

Rides #9 & 10

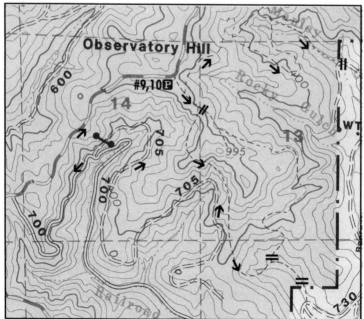

a junction at 1.8 miles. The left fork is the bottom of the stepped track closed to bikes. Option 1 turns back here, ascending the same track you descended.

OPTION 2: Turn right if you want a little more single track descent. Drop through switchbacks left and right, the second one very tight. After another switch left, your track winds right, descending rough tread, then crossing a narrow bridge. After a tiny second bridge down beside Cookhouse Gulch, find a place to turn back. State park property ahead is closed to bikes. You must turn back by wooden post #4 at 2.4 miles. Ride back up the twisting trail, going left at the junction to ascend back up the way you came down.

OPTION 3: At 1.4 miles (or 1 mile from the bottom of Option 2) in the little dip on the ridgetop, find a vague, overgrown track to the right of some redwoods heading northwest. Walk it for 75 feet and drop to the grassy double track of Road 705.

Our count starts from zero here, turning right and ascending moderately on a pleasant roller-coaster track winding through gulches. Watch for the sharp foliage of pampas grass, which cuts with the slightest touch. Descend briefly at .2 mile, then climb gradually to .4 mile. After a brief contour, the double track descends gently, then makes a short steep drop to 1.2 miles. Contour, then dip briefly before a gradual, then moderate uphill to 1.8 miles. Road 705 descends to a wooded gulch at 2.2 miles, then drops to a yellow gate and road's end at 2.4 miles.

Turn right for a steady moderate ascent on Road 700, with an eye out for traffic. At 3.7 miles Road 700 ends at Little Lake Road (Road 408). Turn right on the dirt portion of Road 408 for a gradual ascent and short drop, followed by a steep uphill from 4.2 miles to your starting point at 5 miles.

If you're still game for more challenging single track, this is the start of Ride #9. An easier choice would continue north on Road 408 (Ride #8).

11

Upper Caspar Creek Loop

Jackson State Forest Roads 640 & 630, County Road 408, with options on Roads 600 & 408

This double-track ride starts with an easy contour along a ridge, drops into a creek canyon, then climbs gradually and moderately to gain the next ridge to the north and contour back to your starting point. Technically easy, it's a good workout with several choices to extend your ride.

DIRECTIONS TO STARTING POINT: From the traffic signal on Highway One at M.50.85, head east on Little Lake Road. In 6 miles, where the surface turns to dirt, Little Lake Road is signed "Road 408." Continue 2.1 miles to an unmarked intersection, 8.1 miles from Highway One, where Road 640 on your left ascends behind a yellow gate. Park on the shoulder of Road 408, making sure not to block traffic on either road.

ELEVATION AT START: 960 feet

OPTION 1: Roads 640, 630 and 408.
  Moderate, 9.1-mile loop, little or no vehicle traffic.
  Elevation Gain/Loss: 980 feet+/980 feet-

OPTION 2: Roads 640, 600, 630 and 408.
  Moderate, 9.6-mile loop, little or no vehicle traffic.
  Elevation Gain/Loss: 1140 feet+/1140 feet-

OPTION 3: Add a ride north along part of Road 408, Ride #8.
  Moderate, 5.6 miles round trip to Highway 20, light vehicle traffic.
  Elevation Gain/Loss: Add 1040 feet+/1040 feet- to Highway 20

SURFACE: Dirt state forest roads

MAP: Page 48

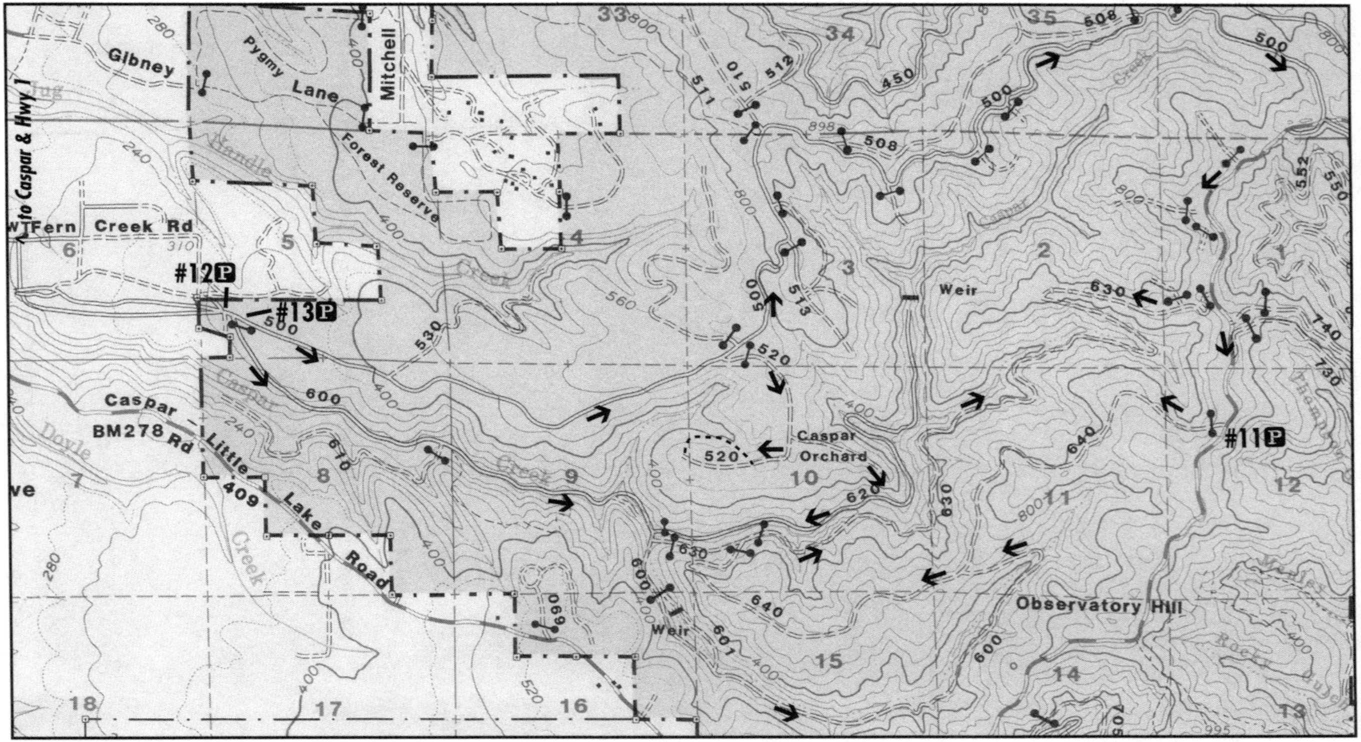
to Caspar & Hwy 1
Gibney
Pygmy Lane
Mitchell
Forest Reserve
Fern Creek Rd
#12P
#13P
Caspar
BM278 Rd
Little Lake Road
409
Caspar Orchard
Weir
Observatory Hill
#11P
530
600
610
500
520
513
511
510
512
450
508
898
552
550
630
740
730
640
620
601
690
705
995

Ride Notes

Ascend gradually on Road 640 as it winds west along the ridge. Reach the summit by .2 mile and start a gentle, then gradual descent. On a clear day you'll have an ocean view around .4 mile. The descent continues to 1.7 miles, where you meet the top end of Road 600 on your left. (**OPTION 2** turns left and descends Road 600 for 2.1 miles, then turns right to ascend Road 630 — see Ride #13 for details.)

Road 640 follows the ridgetop on four short, easy ups and downs. Reach the final top at 2.7 miles, then begin a gradual descent that soon turns moderate. By 3.6 miles you drop steeply to a fork. The left fork leads to Rides #12 and 13, offering more choices to extend your ride. This description takes the right fork and quickly merges with Road 630 as Road 640 ends.

Head east on Road 630 behind a yellow gate, ascending gently with wooded Caspar Creek on your left. Road 630 makes a mostly easy climb at first, but it's interspersed with several short descents across tributary streams. The descents become rare beyond 4.5 miles, but the climb remains mostly gentle.

At 6.6 miles, make the final slight descent, crossing the headwaters of East Fork Caspar Creek. Road 630 switchbacks left and the ascent increases. Your ascent turns moderate around 7.3 miles as water bars transect otherwise good tread. After Road 630 switchbacks right at 7.4 miles, climb to an unmapped junction. Bear right and head northeast and east on better tread, ascending moderately.

As your ascent eases around 8.1 miles, you have a grand view over the canyons of Caspar Creek to the Pacific Ocean on the western horizon. By 8.4 miles the climb turns moderate and you switchback left, heading for a yellow gate.

Beyond the gate Road 630 ends at County Road 408. (For a longer ride, **OPTION 3** turns left on Road 408 — see Ride #8 from 3.2 miles.) Option 1 turns right and follows 408 south on an easy roller coaster run along the ridgetop. Pass two spur roads on the left. The first, Road 740, leads to Old Mill Farm, a working homestead that offers reasonable lodging by reservation (call 707/ 937-0244). The second spur is Road 730. After one last short descent, return to your starting point at 9.1 miles.

12

Caspar Creek Watershed

Jackson State Forest Roads 500 & 520, with options on Roads 600, 620, 630, 640, 408 & single track

The network of state forest roads east of the sleepy town of Caspar offers diverse options: double track ranging from an easy ramble to moderate loops and one fun single track with a steep descent. Despite a recent timber harvest in the area, these rides explore some pretty country, especially down along the creek. Our description starts 1.5 miles from Highway One, but you can extend your ride by starting from the highway or from tiny Caspar.

The recent harvest has disrupted one single track trail popular with the community. In negotiations before the harvest, state forest staff assured community members the trail would survive, but at press time it was impassable. The short fun track forked right from Road 500 .8 mile from the starting point, descended gradually, then down a short steep hill, then roller coastered gently through forest before ending at Road 600 after a mile. I describe it here to urge state forest staff to keep their word to restore it, and to allow you to find it when they do.

DIRECTIONS TO STARTING POINT: Turn east off Highway One at Caspar (M.55.2). In .3 mile turn right on Caspar Orchard Road (Road 410). At .5 mile continue straight on dirt Road 500, which soon turns east. At 1.5 miles from Highway One, park in the broad turnout on the left side of the road.

ELEVATION AT START: 320 feet

OPTION 1: Roads 500, 520 and return.
Easy, 6.8 miles round trip, light vehicle traffic.
Elevation Gain/Loss: 400 feet+/400 feet-

OPTION 2: Roads 500, 520, Orchard Spur, short single track, 620 and 600.
Moderate, 7.1-mile loop, light vehicle traffic.
Elevation Gain/Loss: 610 feet+/610 feet-

OPTION 3: Roads 500, 408, 630 and 600.
            Moderate, 15.5-mile loop, light vehicle traffic.
            Elevation Gain/Loss: 1300 feet+/1300 feet-

OPTION 4: Roads 500, 408, 640, 630 and 600.
            Moderate, 15-mile loop, light vehicle traffic.
            Elevation Gain/Loss: 1310 feet+/1310 feet-

SURFACE: Dirt state forest roads, single track on Option 2

MAP: Page 48

Ride Notes

Ascend east on broad Road 500 (vehicle traffic). At .1 mile Road 600 forks right and descends, your return at the end of Options 2, 3 and 4 (also see Ride #13). Climb steadily on Road 500. At .6 mile, Road 530 forks left behind a yellow gate. (It ends in 1.3 miles at Jughandle Creek.) Road 500 crests the first hill at .8 mile. A short descent passes the single track on the right that was disrupted by 1996 logging. Continue east on Road 500, ascending gradually past several short spur roads. At 2.2 miles a broad turnout on your right marks the start of unmarked Road 520.

    OPTIONS 1 & 2: Turn right on Road 520, a narrow double track which ascends briefly behind a rusty silver gate. Road 520 soon descends gently, bending right to head south at 2.5 miles.

    Ignore several spurs until 2.8 miles, where a double track branches left, the way for Option 2. A tall stump topped with a huckleberry bush stands left of the junction. Option 1 continues on Road 520, descending briefly to a large meadow, site of the Caspar Orchard, which provided fruit for the Caspar Lumber Company cookhouse. Contour along the top of the meadow to 3 miles, then descend slightly through forest. Enter a second meadow at 3.2 miles. At its west end at 3.3 miles, the road splits in two. Take the right fork to circle the meadow's northern edge, passing several narrow tracks into the forest. The fork loops back to the meadow's east side at 3.6 miles. Turn left and ascend back to the Option 2 junction at 4 miles. Option 1 retraces your route back up Road 520, then down Road 500 to your starting point at 6.8 miles.

    OPTION 2: Go left on the narrow track at 2.8 miles. It contours beneath overhanging brush, then descends gradually. By 3 miles a short drop leads to the end of the double track. Continue on single track, where a short moderate climb turns gradual, following a ridgetop. You quickly begin a fun descent, which turns steep as the track narrows around 3.3 miles. Save enough braking power to stop before a wood and metal barrier at 3.4 miles. The single track ends as it drops to Road 620.

Turn right on Road 620 (a left turn contours to road's end in about 1.5 miles). The road descends gradually, then moderately, winding above Caspar Creek. Descend gradually beyond 3.9 miles, passing large red-woods along the pretty creek. Road 620 ends at a rusted silver and orange gate at 4.7 miles.

Road 600 is beyond the gate. Road 630 (end of Option 3) starts south of Caspar Creek (see Rides #11 and 13). Option 2 turns right and follows Road 600 west as it contours, with easy ups and downs, above the north bank of Caspar Creek. From 5.8 miles Road 600 makes a steady gradual ascent, ending at Road 500 at 7 miles. Go left .1 mile to your starting point.

OPTIONS 3 & 4: Continue ascending on broad Road 500 beyond Road 520. By 2.4 miles the hill turns moderate. Ascend gradually to a junction at 3.4 miles. Roads 510 and 511 on the left head in different directions (see Ride #19). Continue a gradual climb to 3.7 miles, where Road 508 on the left offers a traffic-free route on natural tread with more ups and downs. Road 500 contours, then descends gently into a large clearcut. The fitful descent continues to 5.7 miles, where you meet the other end of Road 508. The junction with Road 456 (see Ride #27) is just beyond. Road 500 ascends gently, leaving the massive clearcut around 6.2 miles to contour through lovely forest. A gradual ascent brings you to Road 408 at 6.8 miles (see Ride #8).

Turn right on Road 408 and descend briefly, then ascend gradually to 7.6 miles. Dip and rise to 8 miles and the junction with Road 630. Option 3 turns right and descends a long hill on Road 630. From 12 miles the road makes many short ups and downs as it follows East Fork Caspar Creek. Ascend to Road 630's end at 13.1 miles, then go right on Road 600, making a gentle ascent with a few dips until 600 ends at Road 500 at 15.4 miles. Turn left and go .1 mile to your starting point.

OPTION 4: For a ride .5 mile shorter than Option 3 that stays longer on the ridges, continue south along Road 408 beyond Road 630, con-touring to a junction with unmarked Road 640 at 8.7 miles. Follow 640 as it ascends a ridge behind a yellow gate. The next 3.6 miles is described in detail in Ride #11. After you descend to the fork at 12.3 miles, go left and descend to Road 600 at 12.6 miles. Turn right on Road 600 and follow Caspar Creek downstream, then ascend to the end of Road 600 at 14.9 miles. Go left .1 mile to the starting point.

13

Caspar Creek Canyon

Jackson State Forest Roads 600, 640 & 630, with options on Roads 408, 620, 520, 500 & single track

Much of the prettiest country in the heavily logged Caspar Creek watershed lies down along the creek, where Road 600 and its spurs wind along the still wooded banks. The Caspar Lumber Company began cutting timber here in the 1860s, harvesting virtually the entire watershed by axe and crosscut saw before 1900. After Jackson State Forest was created from Caspar Lumber Company's lands in 1947, the state resumed logging, and it continues today. Fortunately, modern logging practices protect a corridor along year-round streams. That has preserved the riparian corridor explored on this ride and its options.

Road 600 descends to only 40 feet above sea level after one mile, then takes an easy meander through the deep canyon for the next four miles, whether you follow Road 600, 620 or 630. Though the three options described here are moderate to strenuous, if you want an easy ride, just turn back around the 5-mile point instead of ascending the ridges.

DIRECTIONS TO STARTING POINT: Turn east off Highway One at Caspar (M.55.2). In .3 mile turn right on Caspar Orchard Road (Road 410). At .5 mile continue straight on dirt Road 500, which soon turns east. At 1.6 miles from Highway One, park in the broad turnout on the left side of the road. Road 600 starts across from the parking area, descending southeast behind a (usually) locked gate.

ELEVATION AT START: 320 feet

OPTION 1: Roads 600, 640, 630 and 600.
Moderate, 9.9-mile semi-loop, little or no vehicle traffic.
Elevation Gain/Loss: 1240 feet+/1240 feet-

OPTION 2: Roads 600, 630, 408, 640, 630 and 600.
Moderate, 13.7-mile semi-loop, little or no vehicle traffic.
Elevation Gain/Loss: 1450 feet+/1450 feet-

OPTION 3: Roads 600, 620, Caspar Orchard single track, 520, 500. Strenuous, 7.1-mile loop, light to medium vehicle traffic. Elevation Gain/Loss: 610 feet+/610 feet-

SURFACE: Dirt logging roads, single track on Option 3

MAP: Page 48

Ride Notes

Cross Road 500 and descend southeast on Road 600 behind the locked gate. (If the gate is open, expect vehicle traffic.) Descend gradually but steadily for 1.2 miles. A few short spurs on the right descend to the creek. Continue east on Road 600, following Caspar Creek upstream. The road mostly contours, with a few easy ups and downs, until a big junction at 2.3 miles. All options radiate from this junction of three roads. Option 3 takes the first fork on the left, Road 620. Option 2 takes the second left, Option 1 returns that way.

OPTION 1: Pass Road 620 on your left, then cross Caspar Creek to pass Road 630, also on the left. Continue on Road 600, crossing to the south side of South Fork Caspar Creek to head south upstream. For the next 2.5 miles, your track ascends fitfully on deteriorating tread, the ascent broken by six short descents.

Road 600 switchbacks left to cross South Fork Caspar Creek at 4.9 miles, then ascends steadily and moderately to its end at 5.4 miles. Beyond a yellow gate, turn left on ridgetop Road 640 (a right turn offers a longer ride, climbing this ridge to the higher ridge to the east — see Ride #11). After a brief descent, ascend gradually west on good tread, with grand views over Caspar Creek watershed. After reaching your highest point on the ridgetop at 6.2 miles, Road 640 descends moderately. At 7.2 miles, stay left at a fork, dropping to Road 640's end at Road 630. Descend fitfully, heading west to Road 630's end at a yellow gate at 7.5 miles. Turn right and follow your tracks back out Road 600, returning to your starting point at 9.9 miles.

OPTION 2: Take the second left at the 2.3-mile junction. Behind a yellow gate, Road 630 heads east, ascending gently with wooded Caspar Creek on your left. Road 630 makes a generally easy climb at first, but it is interspersed with several short descents across tributary streams. The descents become rare after 3.2 miles, but the climb remains mostly gentle.

At 5.3 miles you cross the headwaters of East Fork Caspar Creek as Road 630 switchbacks left. Your ascent turns moderate around 6 miles as water bars disrupt otherwise good tread. After Road 630 switchbacks right, climb to an unmapped junction. Bear right and head northeast and east on improved tread, ascending moderately.

As your ascent eases around 6.8 miles, you have a grand view over the canyons of Caspar Creek to the Pacific Ocean. By 7.1 miles the climb turns moderate and switchbacks left, heading for a yellow gate.

Beyond the gate Road 630 ends at County Road 408. Turn right and follow 408 south on an easy roller-coaster run along the ridgetop. Road 408 meets unmarked Road 640 at 7.8 miles. Turn right and ascend Road 640 to 8 miles, then descend gradually along the ridgetop to 9.7 miles, where Road 600 forks left. Continue on Road 640, making a gentle roller-coaster run to a final top at 9.7 miles. Descend gradually, then moderately. When Road 640 forks at 10.6 miles, go left and merge with Road 630, which soon ends. Turn right and follow Road 600 back to your starting point at 13.7 miles.

OPTION 3 takes the first fork, behind the rusted silver and orange gate, at the 2.3-mile junction. Road 620 ascends gradually along a wooded stretch of Caspar Creek. The rise is moderate from 3.1 miles, then turns gradual again before it meets the steep single track on the left at 3.6 miles. (For an easy ride you can continue up Road 620 to its end in about 1.5 miles.) The single track, marked uphill by three spi-ralling metal tubes and a redwood blockade, ascends extremely steeply to 3.8 miles. Then a pleasant single track descends fitfully, ending at Road 520 at 4.3 miles. Turn right and make a gentle ascent, coming to Road 520's end at Road 500 at 4.9 miles. Turn left and descend Road 500, returning to the starting point at 7.1 miles.

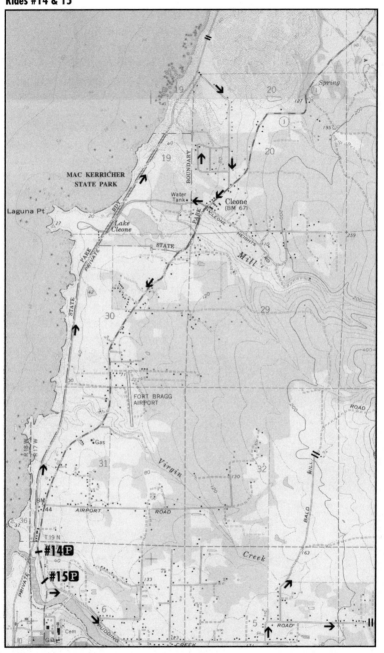

14

MacKerricher State Park

The Haul Road, with options on park roads, Ward Avenue & Highway One

The Haul Road, a former logging truck route between the redwood mill at Fort Bragg and the forests of Ten Mile River, has become a community institution. People of all ages come here from morning until night to walk, bike, jog or wheelchair this nearly level paved track paralleling the park's pristine shore.

A logging railway chugged along this route from 1916 until 1949. Then the rails were paved over and big trucks hauled the logs daily until the winter of 1982, when high tides and storm surf destroyed a mile of the road.

Today you can ride the Haul Road 3.5 miles north, ocean breeze in your face and roar of surf in your ears, to the wave-torn break where a sea of sand dunes lies before you. The parks department plans to lay a bike path across the dunes in 1997 or 1998, once again connecting the road's north and south ends, and allowing a longer ride. Until then the ride is short, easy and well worth the trip. Prolong your excursion by looping along the park roads, riding Ward Avenue, looping through the little town of Cleone, or returning along the busy highway.

DIRECTIONS TO STARTING POINT: Turn west off Highway One at M.62.7 just north of Fort Bragg. Park in the lot left of the silver gate.

ELEVATION AT START: 40 feet

OPTION 1: Haul Road north to washout and return.
Easy, 7 miles round trip.
Elevation Gain/Loss: 60 feet+/60 feet-

OPTION 2: Haul Road to Laguna Point, loop through park and return.
Easy, about 7 miles total, light vehicle traffic.
Elevation Gain/Loss: 100 feet+/100 feet-

OPTION 3: Add Ward Avenue loops.

> Easy, add 1.8-mile Ward loop, 1.7-mile Ward-Cleone-Laguna loop, or 3.6-mile Ward-Highway One loop, light to medium vehicle traffic, except Highway One — heavy traffic.
>
> Elevation Gain/Loss: Ward loop: Add 20 feet+/20 feet-
> > Cleone loop: Add 60 feet+/60 feet-
> > Highway loop: Add 120 feet+/120 feet-

OPTION 4: Add Ride #15.

> Easy, add up to 7.2 miles, light to medium vehicle traffic.
> Elevation Gain/Loss: Add 260 feet+/260 feet-

SURFACE: Paved

FACILITIES: Picnic areas, restrooms, water, phone, campground, store and restaurants in Cleone.

Ride Notes

Please slow to walking speed when passing pedestrians and other users, announcing your presence before you pass from behind, "Cyclist passing on your left."

Beyond the silver gate west of the parking lot, turn right and ride north on the pavement. On your left grassy headlands descend to a rocky tidal zone. Please stay off the highly erodible dirt track there. Though the asphalt is uneven in places, the broad, virtually level road is as easy as a ride gets. At .7 mile the road dips across a rough wooden bridge over Virgin Creek, where a beach of fine sand sometimes drifts across the pavement. Contour north, the rocky intertidal zone close on your left.

By 1.6 miles the Haul Road bisects a corridor lined with shore pines and wax myrtles, where Laguna Point juts seaward to the west. At 1.9 miles one of the park's pleasant campgrounds is on your right. It includes fine, secluded walk-in sites. After you pass a gate, a gravel spur on your left at 2 miles descends to the park road at the Laguna Point parking lot (Option 2 below). The Haul Road crosses another wooden bridge and soon narrows above Cleone Beach on your left and placid Lake Cleone on the right.

At 2.2 miles you come to a short narrow single track where the storm surf swallowed most of the road. Beginners might want to walk this steep-sided single track. All cyclists should yield to pedestrians and equestrians. The Haul Road resumes by 2.3 miles. Soon on your left rocky tidal zones alternate with tiny pocket beaches.

Watch for a dirt break in the pavement at 2.75 miles. After good tread resumes, pass the Ward Avenue access point on the right at 3.15 miles (see Option 3). The Haul Road soon narrows and comes to its storm-ravaged end at 3.5 miles.

A logger once told me you could follow this and connecting haul roads to the Oregon border. Until the bike path extension is built over the dunes, turn back here, unless you enjoy riding deep sand (not recommended!). Before you return, stop to admire the virtual wilderness to your north. A four-mile beach, backed by dunes, stretches to Ten Mile River. To the northeast the river's remote canyons wind toward 4234-foot Cahto Peak. Look northwest to Bruhel Point at the base of grassy Kibesillah Hill, the cliffs of the Lost Coast's Sinkyone Wilderness and King Range jutting beyond (see Rides #35 and 36).

Turn around and head back the way you came, keeping in mind the options at Ward Avenue and Laguna Point.

OPTION 2: Leave the Haul Road at Laguna Point, 2 miles north of the starting point. Beware of motorized traffic as you ride up to 3 miles of paved park roads, looping through forest, meadow and dune and past Lake Cleone, a popular fishing and bird-watching area. Return to the Haul Road where you left it and ride south to your starting point.

OPTION 3: If you leave the Haul Road at Ward Avenue at 3.15 miles, you have three choices to extend your ride. Most simply, go right or left on Ward Avenue to ride the 1.8-mile loop it makes between park and highway, returning on the Haul Road. Or ride Ward Avenue to Highway One, follow the highway .15 mile south, turn right on Mill Creek Drive and follow it through the park to Laguna Point, where you can rejoin the Haul Road for the 2-mile return to your starting point. The third choice stays on the highway at Mill Creek Drive, following the busy road's shoulder 2.5 miles back to your starting point.

OPTION 4: If you've exhausted the options above and still want a longer ride, follow the highway shoulder south .5 mile to Pudding Creek Road, then cross Highway One and follow Pudding Creek Road east, as described in Ride #15.

15

Pudding Creek

Pudding Creek Road, with option on Bald Hill Road

This is a pleasant family ride by itself or a nice addition to a ride on the MacKerricher Haul Road, Ride #14. Following two lightly traveled country lanes north of Fort Bragg to their ends, you go from coastal estuary to rural pasture at the base of Bald Hill, once the eastern boundary of the Mendocino Indian Reservation.

DIRECTIONS TO STARTING POINT: Turn west off Highway One at M.62.3 into the Pudding Creek parking area at the northern edge of Fort Bragg.

ELEVATION AT START: 30 feet

OPTION 1: Pudding Creek Road to end.
Easy, 5 miles round trip, light to medium traffic.
Elevation Gain/Loss: 190 feet+/190 feet-

OPTION 2: Add Bald Hill Road.
Easy, add 2.25 miles round trip, light traffic.
Elevation Gain/Loss: Add 70 feet+/70 feet-

OPTION 3: Add Ride #14, Option 1 on the MacKerricher Haul Road.
Easy, add 7.5 miles round trip.
Elevation Gain/Loss: Add 80 feet+/80 feet-

SURFACE: Paved

FACILITIES: Pit toilet at north end of parking area.

MAP: Page 56

Ride Notes

Ride south from the parking area for .1 mile to where Pudding Creek Road heads east. Cautiously cross Highway One and ride Pudding Creek

Road east. After a short brisk hill, the ascent eases, with views over Pudding Creek on your right. From the stop sign at .4 mile, continue up Pudding Creek Road on an easy ascent. Beyond Petaluma Avenue at 1 mile, the road dips briefly, then resumes its gentle climb.

Pudding Creek Road bends left and right, coming to an intersection with Bald Hill Road at 1.8 miles. You can continue up Pudding Creek to 2.5 miles, where the public road ends at private property. Turn around and descend the way you came.

OPTION 2: At 1.8 miles from Highway One, turn north on Bald Hill Road, which quickly loses its stripe to become a paved but sleepy country lane. Pass through some woods along upper Virgin Creek, then contour through pasture lands. Bald Hill rises on your right. At .6 mile from Pudding Creek a gentle uphill begins, continuing to the end of the paved road and private property at 1.1 miles. Pedal back the way you came.

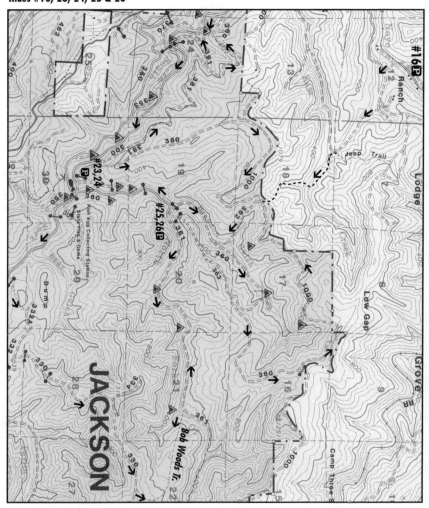

62

16

Company Ranch to Jackass Pass

Little Lake-Sherwood Trail

The ride described in Option 1 is only 2.5 miles in each direction, but two thirds of it is pleasant single track, a rare and highly sought after commodity for experienced mountain bikers. This ride also combines nicely with several other rides, giving you some longer excursions to choose from. A highlight along the route is the pleasant site of the community of Sointula. In a clearing along Kass Creek, during the Great Depression several Finnish-American families established a cooperative community to counter their unemployment by growing their own food and working together for their mutual benefit. No buildings remain, but the site has a special feeling.

DIRECTIONS TO STARTING POINT: Turn east off Highway One onto Oak Street (M.61.3) in Fort Bragg. In one mile, Oak becomes Sherwood Road. Go 4.1 miles more to intersection of Sherwood Road and Company Ranch Road, turn right and descend Company Ranch Road 1.4 miles to a T intersection. The county road ends here and the owners of the Company Ranch do not allow parking on their property. Turn around and park on the shoulder facing Sherwood Road. Do not block the gate. Parking is limited.

ELEVATION AT START: 50 feet

OPTION 1: Little Lake-Sherwood Trail to Jackass Pass and return.
Moderate, 5 miles round trip, little or no vehicle traffic.
Elevation Gain/Loss: 820 feet+/820 feet-

OPTION 2: Little Lake-Sherwood Trail to Highway 20 and return.
Strenuous, 14.2 miles round trip, little or no vehicle traffic.
Elevation Gain/Loss: 2770 feet+/2770 feet-

OPTION 3: Add Ride #24 to Option 1.
Moderate, 11.2 miles total, little or no vehicle traffic.
Elevation Gain/Loss: 1750 feet+ /1750 feet-

OPTION 4: Add Ride #25 to Option 1.
Moderate, 12.7 miles total, little or no vehicle traffic.
Elevation Gain/Loss: 1970 feet+/1970 feet-

SURFACE: Dirt single and double track

FACILITIES: On Options 2 and 3, Camp One has picnic area, pit toilets, phone, trash cans, free camping with permit, but bring your own water.

Ride Notes

From the end of the county road, go right on the road that angles across the Skunk railroad tracks, then fork left on the road across the bridge over North Fork Noyo River. Sometimes the bridge is removed in winter, in which case you can only reach this route from Rides #24 or 25. If the bridge is in, ascend southeast from the river on the oiled track.

At a junction .25 mile from your starting point, turn left on the road signed "No Trespassing, Beware of Dog." Pedal up a short hill, contour through forest, then ascend moderately to .55 mile. On your left, the road you've been following ascends over private property. You want to take the unsigned right fork and descend on the Little Lake-Sherwood Trail. A four-foot wide redwood stump stands to the right of your track at the junction. By .6 mile you are beside a small creek. Follow the single track that turns right to ford the creek and climb a short hill. Your single track contours above a marsh on your right, then ascends southeast up the side canyon. After two dips around 1 mile, ford a seasonal side stream, then continue up single track that zigzags up the winding creek.

After a short steep incline, reach a landing at a big bend on a dirt road at 1.2 miles. Apple trees and daffodils mark the spot. The Finnish-American community called Sointula thrived here in the 1930s. Though several roads and trails head in various directions, the only legal one is our described route along the Little Lake-Sherwood Trail. Go left and follow the main road southeast on a slight descent. By 1.4 miles a small hiker symbol confirms that this is the Little Lake-Sherwood Trail.

Continue along Kass Creek until the road forks at 1.7 miles. Take the right fork and cross the metal bridge over the creek to ascend moderately heading south on double track. Two more hiker symbols mark the route. Around 1.8 miles you can look south to a ridge with a saddle — that notch, called Jackass Pass, is your destination. At 2 miles the road makes a big bend right. Leave the road and veer left on the single track ascending gradually south and southeast. A hiker symbol on a young redwood on your left is hidden by the tree's foliage. The track ascends gradually across a side stream, then left of a quarry at 2.1 miles, continuing southeast. Continue the fitful, winding ascent on gravelly single track. All but advanced riders will want to dismount at 2.3 miles for a steep, rough section of track through a gully. Better tread ascends to its end at 2.5 miles, where you meet Road 1000 at Jackass Pass on the ridge. Option 1 retraces your route from there.

OPTION 2 continues on Little Lake-Sherwood Trail, with no more single track for miles. Across the saddle a hiker symbol and State Forest boundary sign mark the route. It follows Road 362 on a steep, bumpy descent to its end at 3.2 miles. To continue on Little Lake-Sherwood Trail, turn right on Road 360. It drops gently to a big junction at 3.9 miles, then turns right and follows Road 360 over a rise and down the North Fork of South Fork Noyo River. Road 360 ends at 5.1 miles. Cross broad Road 300 and follow Road 350 briefly, then take the first left. Little Lake-Sherwood Trail passes Campsite #2 and ascends a rutted double track to reach Highway 20 at 7.1 miles. This final leg is described in Ride #22. Little Lake-Sherwood Trail continues almost to Mendocino on Roads 500 and 408 south of Highway 20 (Ride #8), but Option 2 retraces your route to your starting point.

OPTIONS 3 & 4 combine double-track loops with Option 1 from the Jackass Pass junction. While you can follow loop Rides #24 or 25 in either direction, the easiest routes follow those rides as described in their texts, namely down Road 362 and up 380 and 360 respectively. See Rides #24 and 25 for details.

Ride #17, west end

Ride #17, east end

66

17

Sherwood Ridge to Willits

Sherwood Road Leg, Little Lake-Sherwood Trail

The Pomo people followed a trail along Sherwood Ridge for centuries. By the 1880s a stagecoach jostled along the widened, barely improved route, carrying passengers between Ukiah and Fort Bragg. After 1911 the California Western Railroad bore most of the traffic along the Noyo River Canyon far below, making Sherwood Road the usually lonesome county right of way it still is today. You're only likely to see much traffic here on summer weekends.

For cyclists this route offers moderate to strenuous rides with abundant ups and downs over remote coastal mountain terrain. This is no place for a short ride unless you love hill climbs — a round trip to the 3-mile point rises and drops 1000 feet. Most of the road traverses private timber lands, so it offers no loops, and the only options are where you turn back. If you arrange a pick up in Willits, you can ride the rugged 37 miles one way. Or spend the night and ride the Skunk Train back the next day. Call CWRR (707/ 964-6371) first and make sure they can carry your bike. Option 4, the best choice for a shorter ride on Sherwood Ridge, starts from the east.

DIRECTIONS TO STARTING POINT: Turn east off Highway One onto Oak Street (M.61.3) in Fort Bragg. Head east on Oak, which becomes Sherwood Road in one mile. Milepost markers count from there. Go 4.1 miles more to the junction of Sherwood Road and Company Ranch Road. Park off road.

WARNING!: Sherwood Road may be extremely muddy in winter and spring, especially the first 3 miles. In summer the eastern half can be hot and dusty. Logging operations sometimes cause delays, but should be clearly posted.

ELEVATION AT START: 580 feet

OPTION 1: Sherwood Road to Coon Camp Rest Stop.
Moderate, 15.4 miles round trip, little or no vehicle traffic.
Elevation Gain/Loss: 1790 feet+/1790 feet-

OPTION 2: Sherwood Road to spring below Sherwood Peak.
Strenuous, 41.6 miles round trip, little or no vehicle traffic.
Elevation Gain/Loss: one way: 3760 feet+/1830 feet-
round trip: 5590 feet+/5590 feet-

OPTION 3: Sherwood Road to Willits on Highway 101.
Strenuous, 37.2 miles one way, little or no vehicle traffic, except
east end — moderate traffic.
Elevation Gain/Loss: one way: 4390 feet+/3490 feet-

OPTION 4: Sherwood Road from east. Drive west from Highway 101 on
Sherwood Road for 12.4 miles to intersection. Ride Sherwood
Road west to spring or 1152-foot saddle.
Moderate, 8 miles round trip to spring, 23 miles round trip to saddle.
Elevation at start: 2300 feet
Elevation Gain/Loss: to spring: 1040 feet+/1040 feet-
to saddle: 2410 feet+/2410 feet-

SURFACE: Dirt county road

FACILITIES: Picnic tables, campsites at Coon and Wanhalla Camps.

Ride Notes

Ride Sherwood Road east, contouring for .7 mile. Then a big bend left
has views east up North Fork Noyo River. Ascend moderately past the
last residence for miles. By 1.2 miles a large clearcut affords views north
over Pudding Creek Canyon and east up the Noyo. Ascend fitfully to
1.5 miles where the vista looks west to Fort Bragg and the Pacific Ocean.
Climb moderately on rutted track to another top at 1.7 miles.

Sherwood Road descends moderately to 2 miles as views switch
south and east. Ascend steeply to 2.4 miles. If this climb is muddy, a
narrower track to your left may be better. Descend fitfully, then contour from 2.7 miles. Look east to see 6873-foot Hull Mountain 40 miles
away in Mendocino National Forest. Drop gradually to a saddle at 3.2
miles. After an easy up-down-up, contour along the ridgetop on better
tread around 3.4 miles. Dip to 3.75 miles, then ascend gradually to 4.1,
followed by a gentle down-up-down to a broad landing before 4.5 miles.

The easy trend continues with a mile-long gradual uphill interrupted
by one brief descent. After a short contour, descend moderately around
a clearcut for .3 mile. This leads to a junction with two private roads on
your left at 6 miles. Ascend gradually to 6.8 miles, then moderately
through another clearcut. From 7 miles, your track drops moderately
to a saddle at 7.7 miles.

A corral on the right is for nearby Coon Camp, a Little Lake-Sherwood Trail Rest Stop with a picnic table beside redwoods. Hikers and equestrians have priority to camp there, but since it's seldom used, cyclists might stay overnight. Brackish spring water nearby should be purified before drinking, also advisable at a better spring .5 mile ahead. Option 1 returns from here.

OPTIONS 2 & 3: Sherwood Road makes a long ascent, gradual to 8.1 miles, then moderate past the spring and a seasonal creek to 9 miles. Then a fitful, mostly gradual ascent, broken by a short drop around 10.5 miles, continues to 11.5 miles, where you top 1600 feet. Contour along the ridgetop past junctions on your left with Ramsey Ridge Road and another around 11.9 miles (M.16). Sherwood Road continues east on a fitful ascent to a ridgetop knob at 12.5 miles, where a recent fire scarred twin redwoods on your left. Dip and rise to a summit of 1750 feet before 12.8 miles.

Your route descends to 1420 feet around 14.1 miles, passing M.18.25, the last county road marker for 12 miles. Ascend to a junction at 14.5 miles. Sherwood Road turns northwest, climbing past Marble Place. Dip and rise before a long descent as the road turns north. Drop to a saddle (1152 feet) around 16.5 miles, then follow the ridgetop on an ascending trend with dips and rises. Pass Wanhalla Camp south of the road around 17 miles.

A long moderate ascent heads toward Sherwood Peak. At 20.8 miles a clear stream bubbles from the mountainside beside the road in a pleasant shady spot. At elevation 2400 feet, it offers a great break before you turn back (Option 2) or continue east.

OPTION 3 continues east, ascending moderately along the flank of 3209-foot Sherwood Peak. Cross a ridge running south at 21.4 miles, with views east to the 7000-foot Yolla Bollys and west to the coast on clear days. Ascend to the road's summit — 2870 feet — at 22.4 miles. Sherwood Road drops gradually, then steeply by sharp curves with some rough tread. The road levels in Sherwood Valley and passes Octagon House at 24.5 miles, official end of Little Lake-Sherwood Trail. Sherwood Road turns right at a junction at 24.8 miles. Pick up pavement and traffic as you contour through Sherwood Valley, passing the final milepost from Fort Bragg, M.30.26, at 26.2 miles. Continue past a junction with a fork left to Laytonville at 26.7 miles. It's mostly downhill to Sherwood Road's end at Highway 101 in Willits, except for sharp ascents around 28 and 32 miles. Pass a small store around 34 miles and drop steeply to road's end at Highway 101, 37.2 miles from your starting point.

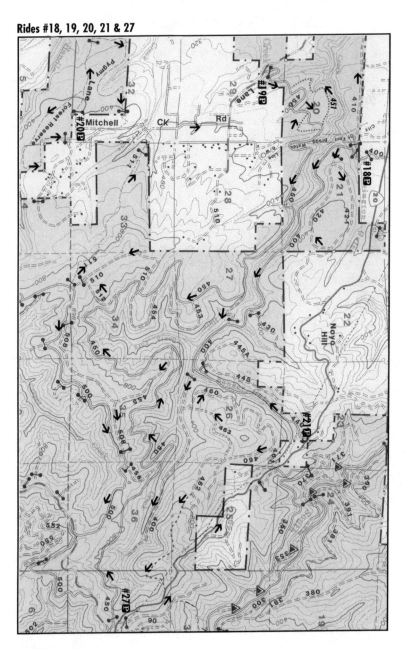

18

Hare Creek Canyon

Jackson State Forest Road 400, with options on Roads 410, 420 & 421

One of the gentlest rides in Jackson State Forest, this ramble along the canyon of Hare Creek makes an ideal family excursion. Much of Road 400 follows the route of the Caspar Lumber Company Railroad, thus the easy grade. The ride's proximity to Fort Bragg, its link with two other rides (#19 and 21), and the short but pleasantly challenging track of Option 3 make this a great choice for a short or long excursion.

DIRECTIONS TO STARTING POINT: Turn east off Highway One at M.59.8 onto Highway 20. Go 2.3 miles, then turn right onto Gravel Pit Road. Go .1 mile to road fork. Road 400 is on the right behind the yellow gate. Do not block gate when parking.

ELEVATION AT START: 320 feet

OPTION 1: Road 400 to Road 450 connector.
  Easy, 6.5 miles round trip, little or no vehicle traffic.
  Elevation Gain/Loss: 460 feet+/460 feet-

OPTION 2: Road 400 to end.
  Easy, 10.2 miles round trip, little or no vehicle traffic.
  Elevation Gain/Loss: 530 feet+/530 feet-

OPTION 3: Add Road 421/420 loop.
  Moderate, add 3.5-mile loop, no vehicle traffic.
  Elevation Gain/Loss: Add 280 feet+/280 feet-

OPTION 4: Add Road 410
  Easy, add 2.1 miles round trip, little or no vehicle traffic.
  Elevation Gain/Loss: Add 160 feet+/160 feet-

SURFACE: Dirt roads

Ride Notes

Pass the yellow gate and descend moderately on good tread. Stay left at the first junction. The right fork is Road 410 (Option 4), which heads west to end in just over one mile. Road 400 drops steeply to cross the healthy stream of Covington Gulch, then contours southeast following Hare Creek upstream.

At .5 mile stay to the right at an intersection. The left fork climbs moderately past a locked gate, leading to the Road 421/420 loop (see Option 3). Continue on Road 400 as it contours along pretty Hare Creek on your right. It's an easy ride, mostly on narrow double track, with a few short climbs and dips to add variety.

At 3.25 miles you come to an intersection where a road enters on the right. This is the Road 450 connector, which crosses Hare Creek and ascends to Road 450 in .5 mile, 4 miles from Simpson Lane. Make that brisk 150-foot climb if you want to link with Ride #19. Or turn around here to complete an easy 6.5-mile ride.

OPTION 2: Road 400 continues its easy run along Hare Creek nearly to the headwaters. This leg mostly follows the track bed of Caspar Lumber Company's logging railroad, a segment built before 1890. At 3.9 miles Road 440 is on your left. Be careful after the junction — a wooden bridge has holes big enough to swallow a bike tire. Road 400 contours upstream. Stay right at 4.1 miles, where 460 forks left (see Ride #21). Road 400 continues on a slight incline, with a couple of dips and rises around 4.7 miles.

At 5.1 miles the double track ends. A rough and narrow single track continues upstream, but it ends in .2 mile. This last stretch is really too rough for a good ride. Consider parking your bike and sauntering up the trail to stretch your leg muscles before the ride back. If you do, watch for poison oak and big spotted salamanders — you wouldn't want to squash any of the remaining local residents.

OPTION 3: For a shorter, more challenging ride, or to extend the easy ride with more rigorous terrain and track, take the uphill track at the intersection .5 mile from the starting point. Behind a gate this road begins as an overgrown, eroded double track ascending moderately. By .1 mile go left at a fork on unmarked Road 421 (you'll return on the right — Road 420). Road 421 ascends gently with a few dips and a couple of short, steeper climbs. Ignore several vague forks on the right and stay on the main track until an obvious fork around 1 mile. There the left fork heads east onto private property, so take the right fork (Road 420), which heads south on a gentle ascent. Your track contours, then turns west to dip and rise. Descend fitfully on uneven tread, returning to the 420/421 junction at 3.4 miles. Turn left and descend to Road 400.

OPTION 4: ·For a short easy side trip, turn right at the first junction after the starting point. Unmarked Road 410 ascends briefly to a yellow gate, then contours west along a terrace above Hare Creek. The track rises slightly, then descends gradually to its end just over 1 mile from the gate. As you return, you might investigate several short single track spurs that head toward the creek.

19

Hare Creek Watershed

Jackson State Forest Road 450, with options on Roads 451, 510, 511, 400, Mitchell Creek Drive, Simpson Lane, Highway 20 & Highway One

This broad double-track logging road offers plenty of variety: easy riding, a challenging climb and descent, short and fun single track, connections with other rides, and last but not least, a cycling practice pit. Being close to town, it is one of the most popular areas in Jackson State Forest, but I've also had the entire place to myself. Watch for equestrians, walkers and other bikers, including the motorized kind.

Only .3 mile from Simpson Lane, watch on your left for a small cycling practice pit. This tiny network of hills, turns, dips and moguls offers a warm up for the single track ahead.

DIRECTIONS TO STARTING POINT: South of Fort Bragg, turn east off Highway One onto Simpson Lane (M.59.3). Go 1.9 miles, then turn left to unmarked Road 450, where you park (do not block gate).

ELEVATION AT START: 330 feet

OPTION 1: Road 450, single track and return.
Easy, 3-mile semi-loop, little or no vehicle traffic.
Elevation Gain/Loss: 220 feet+/220 feet-

OPTION 2: Roads 450, 451 and return.
Easy, 3.2-mile semi-loop, little or no vehicle traffic.
Elevation Gain/Loss: 270 feet+/270 feet-

OPTION 3: Roads 450, 510, 511, Mitchell Creek Road, Simpson Lane.
Moderate, 10.8-mile loop, little or no vehicle traffic, except on paved roads — medium traffic.
Elevation Gain/Loss: 1310 feet+/1310 feet-

OPTION 4: Roads 450 and 400, Highway 20, Highway One, Simpson Lane.
Moderate 13-mile round trip or 12.5-mile loop, little or no vehicle traffic, except on paved roads — heavy traffic.
Elevation Gain/Loss: round trip: 1170 feet+/1170 feet-; loop: 860 feet+/860 feet-

SURFACE: Dirt logging roads. Option 3 involves residential streets. Option 4 loop has highway riding.

MAP: Page 70

Ride Notes

Behind the metal gate, descend the broad road, winding across two tributaries of Hare Creek. After the second stream, navigate loose sand, then ascend briefly. Resume a gentle descent, crossing another feeder for Hare Creek. At 1.3 miles, pass the start of Option 2 on the left. The descent on Road 450 soon steepens, rounding a big bend to the right.

OPTION 1: Unless you're an advanced rider, dismount at 1.4 miles to lift your bike up to a narrow single track. Contour south along a ridge through forest. At 1.7 miles, turn right onto another single track (the first track quickly dead-ends at private property). Make a fun, easy drop off the ridge, returning to Road 450 at 1.8 miles. If you return from here, it's a 3-mile loop.

OPTION 2: At 1.3 miles from Simpson Lane, the start of Road 451 is obscured by large stumps. Take a narrow path left of the stumps to find a track that descends, then roller coasters gently through forest. After crossing a lush tributary of Hare Creek at 2 miles, duck under low branches as you dip and rise some more. At a broad clearing at 2.25 miles, a steep spur drops to Hare Creek. The bike route veers left to ascend steeply, then moderately, returning to Road 450 at 2.5 miles. Turn right to return to your starting point at 3.2 miles.

OPTION 3: Continue along Road 450 past the first two spurs. The road narrows and descends moderately, then gradually over water bars. After crossing a stream, ascend moderately past 2 miles, then drop to a stream at 2.7 miles. Climb a long uneven hill through a clear cut with views on your left across Hare Creek to dense forest on its north bank. The tread improves before the ascent ends around 3.5 miles. After a brief down-up-down, your track resumes a gentle ascent.

Pass a yellow gate at 4 miles and come to a junction. The numberless road on the left descends to cross Hare Creek and meet Road 400 in .5 mile (Option 4). Road 450 veers right and makes the steepest ascent so far. The junction is a good place to take a break, or turn back if an 8-mile ride is enough for today.

Continuing on Road 450, the steep ascent soon turns moderate. From 4.5 miles, alternate between easy descents and climbs of varying severity until the marked junction at 6 miles. Where the road forks, Road 450 veers left to descend. (It drops toward Hare Creek, then ascends the creek's headwaters, ending at Highway 20 in about 8 miles — see Ride #27.) Our description forks right on Road 510, which ascends gradually on even tread. Other than a couple of short, steep climbs, this is one of the most pleasant stretches on this loop.

Gain the summit at 6.7 miles, topping a ridge just east of the top of Mitchell Creek Peak (960 feet). Watch for bumps in otherwise smooth tread as you contour along the ridge through gentle dips and rises. After a rusty gate at 7.1 miles, disregard forks right, then left (descends to Road 450) to continue on mostly even tread.

Road 510 ends at Road 500 (see Ride #12, Options 3 and 4) at 7.25 miles. Many choices are possible here in the heart of the Mendocino coast backwoods. Our described loop makes a sharp right onto unmarked Road 511, which descends past a yellow gate blocked by large boulders. Be ready for an exciting descent marked by narrow tunnels through brush and sporadic stretches of deeply eroded and uneven tread.

Sit back and keep the brakes handy descending Road 511's rough, sometimes narrow tread. Drop steeply toward Mitchell Creek around 7.5 miles, watching for bumps and ruts. At 7.8 miles navigate some deep gullies and brush. Slow for deeply grooved tread around 8 miles. Glide through patches of loose sand, then ascend briefly on narrow tread. Resume the steady descent by 8.3 miles, dropping through rough tread at 8.7 miles, then ducking under a low manzanita. After more loose sand, the tread improves for a variable descent on white clay. After a short rise at 9 miles, resume your descent, soon shooting a narrow gauntlet of manzanita.

Before 9.3 miles the tread turns very rough. Nasty thorned blackberry vines hang in the path. Descend steeply through sharp bends left and right. From 9.4 miles, consider walking your bike on the last .1 mile to pavement. Hazards here include deeply grooved tread, a nasty sandstone shelf, and a dangerous washout at the crossing of Mitchell Creek. Come to road's end at paved Mitchell Creek Drive.

Turn right to complete the loop, watching for traffic. After a brief climb, contour along pavement through a neighborhood. Where Mitchell Creek Drive ends at 10.2 miles, turn left and descend Simpson Lane .6 mile to your starting point.

OPTION 4: Go left at the junction at 4 miles and descend across Hare Creek, meeting Road 400 at 4.5 miles. See Ride #18 for a complete description. If you turn right, Road 400 ends in 2 miles. You can loop back to your starting point by turning left on Road 400 and contouring downstream on an easy run. Then Road 400 turns north and ascends moderately to a yellow gate at 7.75 miles. Pass the gate and go .1 mile to Highway 20, then turn left and ride the busy highway's shoulder 2.3 miles to Highway One. Go left on the highway .5 mile to Simpson Lane and turn left, picking up a bike lane to ascend gradually back to your starting point in 1.9 miles, a loop of 12.5 miles.

20

Pygmy Forest Reserve

Gibney Fire Road with loop options

This easy 7.6-mile double loop offers some pleasant and unusual scenery in the Pygmy Forest Reserve of Jackson State Forest. The ride is adjacent to the Jughandle State Reserve, which is off limits to bikes. In the Pygmy Forest you'll see mature dwarf trees — 3 to 6 feet tall — caused by acidic hardpan soils extremely deficient in nutrients. Dwarf species include Bishop and Bolander pines, Mendocino cypress, even a few redwoods. Terrain is gentle on these old logging roads, but significant erosion has created gullies and sand traps that provide mild technical challenge.

DIRECTIONS TO STARTING POINT: South of Fort Bragg, turn east off Highway One onto Simpson Lane (M.59.3). Go 2.5 miles, then turn right onto Mitchell Creek Drive and go 1.5 miles. Your starting point is the silver gate on the right where the paved road turns sharply left. Do not block gate when you park.

ELEVATION AT START: 460 feet

OPTION 1: Gibney Fire Road to Pygmy Forest and return.
Easy, 4 miles round trip, double track.
Elevation Gain/Loss: 170 feet+/170 feet-

OPTION 2: Gibney Fire Road, Mitchell Creek Fire Road, Mitchell Creek Drive.
Easy, 4.7-mile loop, double track with some single track, no vehicle traffic except on Mitchell Creek Drive — light traffic.
Elevation Gain/Loss: 270 feet+/270 feet-

OPTION 3: Gibney Fire Road, Jughandle watershed loop.
Easy, add 2.5-mile loop (or do as separate ride), double track with short single track segment.
Elevation Gain/Loss: Add 200 feet+/200 feet-

SURFACE: Dirt, double track with some single track

MAP: Page 70

Ride Notes

From the silver gate at the big bend, Gibney Fire Lane heads west on a gentle descent, passing several spur roads. At .4 mile, the second spur on the left is Option 3. Gibney continues west on a moderate descent. In several spots you'll encounter rough tread and a few patches of loose sand (actually ancient sand dunes uplifted from the floor of the Pacific!).

After 2 miles you are in the heart of the Pygmy Forest. At a main junction marked by a sea of loose sand (in winter, sometimes a sea of standing water), turn right. (A left turn leads onto state park land, closed to bikes; the road straight ahead is Gibney Fire Road, which comes out on Gibney Lane after passing through some private property.)

Immediately after you turn right, a footpath on your right makes a short loop through the heart of the Pygmy Forest — please don't take your bike on the footpath's sensitive terrain. For the shortest ride (Option 1), turn back and retrace your route for a 4-mile round trip.

OPTION 2: From the junction, contour north on a broad white way, encountering a large pothole or two that may hold standing water into summer — you can walk or ride around the edge, usually on the right. At 2.5 miles you come to a "T" intersection. Turn right and climb sporadically on uneven tread through a pretty forest above the south bank of Mitchell Creek. Before 3 miles descend, then contour through a cypress swamp. By 3.6 miles, ascend gradually, then moderately.

At 3.9 miles a dead-end spur on your right leads to a swampy area where tiny insectivorous sundew plants grow, offering a short side trip. The main track continues its halting ascent, soon coming to a confusing intersection. Go straight or angle right diagonally from here. All the other tracks either dead-end or lead to private property. If you take a viable fork you'll quickly come to Mitchell Creek Drive. Turn right (watch for traffic!) and sprint the skinny side of a mile to your starting point.

OPTION 3: To extend your ride (or for a shorter loop that stands alone), head west on Gibney Fire Road. This time take the second left, at .4 mile, a diagonal that cuts southeast, paralleling Jughandle Creek through another corner of the Pygmy Forest Reserve. This eroded double track ascends gradually through pygmy forest, with tall forest along the creek on your right. At .9 mile a sand trap slows progress at the base of a short moderate hill. After the track bends right, it passes through areas often swampy in winter and spring. If so, please walk your bike. The path narrows to single track in several parts of its east end. Ascend over a ridge at 1.3 miles, then descend briefly before climbing again. Around 1.6 miles, ascend moderately on single track through pleasant forest along the brink of Jughandle Creek's canyon.

By 1.7 miles the path turns north, widening to climb a short steep hill. Pause at the top to admire the best view on this ride. Descend moderately on broad rough tread. The track bends left along the state forest boundary for a short ascent west at 1.9 miles, then descends with an ocean view. If you smell a barnyard, your olfactory sense is confirmed at 2 miles, where vague grassy tread passes a pungent menagerie. At the corner of the farmer's field at 2.1 miles, turn right on vague track climbing north. It soon improves, descending slightly or contouring to its end at Mitchell Creek Drive. Turn left and descend .1 mile to your starting point.

21

Bunker Gulch and Bunker Hill

Jackson State Forest Roads 440 & 400, with options on Roads 460, 462, 463 & single track

This ride starts by dropping 300 feet down to Hare Creek in 1.5 miles, requiring a steep climb at the end of Options 1 and 2, which return this way. At Hare Creek you can choose from easy, moderate or advanced options in the upper Hare Creek watershed. Option 1 offers the prettiest choice, while Option 3 requires a steep ascent to 1100 feet elevation followed by a hairy descent. On maps the hills east of Bunker Gulch have no names, but Bunker Hill has an all-American sound.

In Bunker Gulch the Caspar Lumber Company railroad left Hare Creek via a tunnel built by Chinese labor in 1903. The shaft passed beneath the ridge now occupied by Highway 20 to reach the Noyo River to the north.

DIRECTIONS TO STARTING POINT: Turn east off Highway One at M.59.8 onto Highway 20. Go 5.5 miles to a broad turnout on your right. The turnout leads to Road 440 behind a yellow gate.

WARNING!: Option 3 was being disrupted by logging operations at press time. Inquire before going.

ELEVATION AT START: 520 feet

OPTION 1: Road 440 and Road 400 upper end.
Easy, 6.2 miles round trip, little or no vehicle traffic.
Elevation Gain/Loss: 520 feet+/520 feet-

OPTION 2: Roads 440, 400, 460 and 463.
Moderate, 7-mile semi-loop, little or no vehicle traffic.
Elevation Gain/Loss: 810 feet+/810 feet-

OPTION 3: Roads 440, 400, 460, 462, skid trail and Highway 20.
Advanced, 8.3-mile loop, little or no vehicle traffic.
Elevation Gain/Loss: 1310 feet+/1310 feet-

SURFACE: Dirt logging roads. Option 3 has steep single track and 2 miles on Highway 20.

MAP: Page 70

Ride Notes

Behind the yellow gate, Road 440 descends steeply, then moderately. By .6 mile you descend gradually along the bottom of Bunker Gulch. At 1.5 miles Road 440 ends at Road 400. Turn left and cross the wooden bridge over Bunker Gulch, then follow Hare Creek upstream. Come to another junction by 1.7 miles.

OPTION 1: The easiest choice bears right on Road 400, following the gentle grade of Hare Creek upstream. The track ends at 3.1 miles — see Ride #18 for details. Retrace your route to the starting point.

OPTION 2 goes left at the 1.7-mile junction, ascending Road 460. Take the left fork at the next junction, at 1.8 miles. This option returns by the right fork. Ascend fitfully along Road 460, overlooking Bunker Gulch on your left. Reach the first summit at 2.6 miles. Road 460 dips and climbs four times in the next mile, then climbs in earnest.

After reaching the top of the hill, descend to an unmarked junction, with three choices, at 4.3 miles. Option 2 takes the shortest route, going right on Road 463. It contours briefly, then descends gradually to 4.7 miles on mostly good tread with a few rough spots. Your descent turns steep, easing before it returns to the junction with Road 460 at 5.2 miles. Go straight, then retrace your route up Bunker Gulch, returning to your starting point at 7 miles.

OPTION 3 continues straight at the 4.3-mile junction, contouring on Road 462. Just beyond 4.8 miles, turn right on the road/skid trail that ascends southeast. (Road 462 dead-ends in .7 mile.) This unnumbered road climbs gradually, with two steep hills, through an area scheduled for logging in summer 1996. Narrowing track dips around 5.4 miles, then rises steeply to a top of 1105 feet at 5.6 miles. You can see the ocean from this Bunker Hill on a clear day. A fork splits left to drop north very steeply on duff tread. The main track turns southeast on a moderate, then steep descent, ending at an old road at 5.9 miles. Turn left and ascend gradually on the grassy double track, coming to Highway 20 at 6.2 miles. Turn left and follow the highway shoulder for 2.1 miles. It contours and descends before climbing briefly to meet Road 440 and your starting point at 8.3 miles.

22

Camp One Loop

Steep, challenging single track

Single track that's legal for bikes is a premium commodity and this ride has some of the raddest, most unforgiving single track in the book. If you think you're ready for this challenging ride, try the lower loop, Option 1, first. Then, if you're pumped for an even wilder descent, ascend the nineteenth century Camp One wagon road to the top near Highway 20 and try the upper loop, which drops 600 feet in a twisting descent of only a mile.

If you'd rather not risk it, the Camp One wagon road that forms the eastern side of the loop is part of the Little Lake-Sherwood Trail. The double track is steep but forgiving, ascending 700 feet from Road 350 to reach Highway 20 in 1.3 miles. From there, Ride #27 is just south across Highway 20, with sections of Rides #8 and 28 close by.

Camp One was a Caspar Lumber Company town from 1903 until 1945, with its own store, school, cookhouse, bungalows and bunkhouses, plus a railroad engine house and switching yard, all moved or dismantled when the railroad shut down.

DIRECTIONS TO STARTING POINT: Turn east off Highway One onto Highway 20 at M.59.8, just south of Fort Bragg. Go 5.9 miles to Road 350 on left, leading downhill by some redwoods. In .3 mile, take the right fork. In 2.9 miles from the highway, you approach Camp One and the Noyo Egg-Collecting Station on your left. Park in the small parking area on your left just before the station or in a larger turnout on your right just beyond.

WARNING!: Go slow on this steep narrow track, both to keep your body intact, and to watch for hikers. Misuse of trails can lead to their closure for cycling.

ELEVATION AT START: 140 feet

OPTION 1: Camp One short loop, double and single track.
Moderate, .7-mile loop, technically difficult, not for beginners.
Elevation Gain/Loss: 110 feet+/110 feet-

OPTION 2:   Camp One double loop, double and single track.
Advanced, 3.4-mile double loop. Technically difficult, skilled
riders only.
Elevation Gain/Loss: 730 feet+/730 feet-

SURFACE: Dirt, mostly single track

FACILITIES: Pit toilets, picnic area, phone, trash cans. Camping is free at Camp
One, permit required, bring your own water.

Ride Notes

A well marked trailhead lies across the road from the first parking area.
But for cyclists this ride unfolds better in the reverse direction. So ride
east on Road 350 from the marked trailhead. In .1 mile veer right on
the road beyond the picnic area and outhouse, then veer right again
toward Campsite #2. Look for the trail sign between the camp and the
outhouse on the left.

Ascend moderately on an old double track, the original wagon road
to Camp One. It's rutted, but you can navigate the gullies by riding
skillfully. At .3 mile a sign marks the single track trail of the lower loop.
The Little Lake-Sherwood Trail continues up the wagon road, coming
to Highway 20 at 1.3 miles.

OPTION 1:   For a short ride turn right and descend steeply, watching
for logs, roots and trees along the very narrow, winding track across
steep and unforgiving terrain. At .5 mile you meet the junction with
the upper loop. A wooden trail map there depicts the trail. Descend
moderately, ducking under a low limb and come to loop's end by .65
mile, where you'll want to walk your bike over the tiny raised bridge to
return to Road 350.

OPTION 2:   Did you like that? If so, start to do it over again. But when
you get to the junction of the wagon road and the lower loop (.3 mile
on first loop, 1 mile on double loop), this time stay on the double track
and ascend steadily and steeply to a ridgetop at 1.5 miles. Contour,
then descend briefly.

The route changes to narrow single track, tunneling through Scotch
broom and climbing moderately. Watch for big water bars and berry
vines in the path. Your track broadens at 1.7 miles, then meets a gravel
road. After 100 feet on the road, veer right onto single track and ascend
steeply to 1.9 miles where you meet broad Road 90.

The loop goes right (Little Lake-Sherwood Trail turns left and climbs gently to Highway 20 at 2.2 miles), following Road 90 on a gentle descent to a landing at 2.3 miles. On your right, to the left of two large redwoods, the narrow single track of the upper loop drops steeply east, then bends left around a tall burned redwood stump. Beyond 2.4 miles descend steeply through tight double switchbacks to the head of a gulch with a seasonal stream.

Wind sharply right and contour briefly, then descend moderately on narrow track, easing over wooden speed bumps. At 2.5 miles a short contour across a steep slope ends with a steep drop off the lip of a slip out. Shoot a narrow corridor between a tanoak and a fallen log, contour briefly on a ridgetop, then bend right and drop across slippery oak leaves. After a short but tricky up, descend, then rise again to drop through the heart of a redwood circle.

Descend steeply to a gulch crossing beyond 2.7 miles. The track bends left and heads down the bottom of the gulch. You may need to dismount to cross several narrow bridges across the stream. Veer right and ascend fitfully away from the creek, then drop briefly to the lower loop junction and map at 3.2 miles. Go left and drop to your starting point at 3.4 miles. Whew!

Ride #22

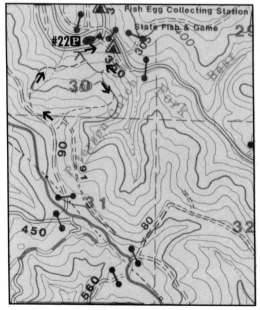

23

North Slope, South Fork Noyo River

Jackson State Forest Roads 380, 381, 391 & 300, with option on 390

Choose from two loops, easy or moderate, traversing several gulches above the South Fork Noyo River, and returning on level track along the river. These pleasant rides can be combined with Ride #24, a more strenuous choice with the same starting point. Or if you're ready for challenging single track, return to nearby Camp One for Ride #22. Consider staying a night or two around Camp One, because you'll find many miles of single and double track in a five-mile radius.

DIRECTIONS TO STARTING POINT: Turn east off Highway One onto Highway 20 at M.59.8, south of Fort Bragg. Go 5.9 miles to Road 350 on the left. In .3 mile, take the right fork. In 3 miles from Highway 20, pass the Noyo Egg-Collecting Station at Camp One. Continue to a big intersection at 3.2 miles. Go left on Road 300 across a wood-surfaced bridge, turn right and park.

ELEVATION AT START: 150 feet

OPTION 1: Roads 380, 381, 391 and 300.
Easy, 5.3-mile loop, little or no vehicle traffic.
Elevation Gain/Loss: 320 feet+/320 feet-

OPTION 2: Roads 380, 381, 390 and 300.
Moderate, 6.8-mile loop, little or no vehicle traffic.
Elevation Gain/Loss: 500 feet+/500 feet-

SURFACE: Dirt logging roads

FACILITIES: Picnic area, pit toilets, phone, trash cans at Camp One. Free camping with permit in Camp One area, but bring your own water.

MAP: Page 62

Ride Notes

Take Road 380 heading west and ascend briefly past a yellow gate. Where Road 380 swings right to climb north after .1 mile, watch for the left fork, Road 381, which contours northwest. The double track ascends gradually on smooth tread for nearly a mile, then descends briefly with views over the canyon of the South Fork Noyo River. The road narrows and becomes rougher as it climbs gently again to 2.2 miles. Descend slightly to a landing overlooking the canyon and the high hills beyond.

The road turns north and drops gradually to an intersection at 2.6 miles. Road 391 on the left offers the easiest option, descending along a seasonal creek. Road 381 offers a longer and more challenging ride of moderate and steep ascents on rough tread.

OPTION 1: Go left on Road 391, descending gradually through lush vegetation above the creek. The continuous descent turns moderate, then reverts to gradual before Road 391 ends at another dirt road before 3 miles. Turn left and descend past a gate to meet Road 300 at 3.3 miles.

Broad Road 300 stays nearly level on mostly excellent tread winding along the South Fork of the Noyo. Enjoy the river views and watch for traffic as you pedal the 2 miles back to your starting point for a 5.3-mile loop.

OPTION 2: If you stay on Road 381, rough tread immediately makes a steep ascent. But the bumpy tread is the only thing consistent about this stretch. After the steep climb, contour briefly, then drop, climb and drop to cross a tributary stream. Ascend steeply again only to drop and climb once more to 3.5 miles, where the road forks. On the right Road 381 rises steeply on rough, loose tread to leave the state forest.

Stay left on Road 390, descending moderately on rough tread. Drop to another intersection at 3.8 miles. Veer left to descend moderately, interrupted by a short easy ascent, all the way to 4.4 miles where you meet Road 391. Go straight on better tread and descend past a gate to meet Road 300 around 4.8 miles. Watch for traffic as you contour along the river, returning to your starting point at 6.8 miles.

24

South Fork Noyo, Ridge Loop

Jackson State Forest Roads 380, 1000, 362, 360 & 300, with optional loops

This loop offers a vigorous workout on the 2-mile ascent, then a ridgetop run with expansive views. A short steep descent leads to a mostly level cruise back to your starting point. Worthwhile options combine this ride with all or part of Rides #16, 23, 25 or 26.

DIRECTIONS TO STARTING POINT: Same as Ride #23.

ELEVATION AT START: 150 feet

OPTION 1: Roads 380, 1000, 362 and 360.
Moderate, 6.2-mile loop, little or no vehicle traffic.
Elevation Gain/Loss: 930 feet+/930 feet-

OPTION 2: Add Ride #16 down to North Fork Noyo River and back.
Moderate, add 5 miles round trip, little or no vehicle traffic, 68% single track.
Elevation Gain/Loss: Add 820 feet+/820 feet-

OPTION 3: Add Ride #25.
Moderate, add 6.3-mile loop, little or no vehicle traffic.
Elevation Gain/Loss: Add 1060 feet+/1060 feet-

OPTION 4: Add all or part of Ride #26.
Easy for Option 1, strenuous for rest, add up to 9.1 miles.
Elevation Gain/Loss: Add 1230 feet+/1230 feet- for loop

SURFACE: Dirt logging roads, with single track on Options 2 and 4.

FACILITIES: Camp and picnic sites in Camp One area, pit toilets, phone and trash cans, but no water.

MAP: Page 62

Ride Notes

Take the road that ascends to and beyond a yellow gate. At .1 mile go right at the fork (Road 381 is on left, see Ride #23). Climb moderately along a ridge on Road 380's rough tread. Numerous water bars hinder your steady ascent. Ignore the numerous side roads, logging skid trails that leave the ridgetop. Gain a knob at 1 mile, then contour to 1.2 miles.

Resume ascending gradually, then moderately, except for a short dip at 1.4 miles. At 1.8 miles a short, steep hill topped by a deep water bar will steal your momentum. The road bends right, leaving the ridgetop and rising steeply to a higher ridge. Gain the main ridgetop, veer right and follow the better tread of Road 1000 on a gradual ascent with grand views north over North Fork Noyo River and Pudding Creek watersheds to Cahto Peak beyond. Top out at 960 feet, descend, then climb to another top at 2.3 miles. Road 1000 descends, then climbs briefly to a final top at 2.7 miles.

As you descend from the last top, keep to the left to avoid the worst of the deep water bars that cut the road's right side. The moderate descent continues to the saddle called Jackass Pass at 3.9 miles, where you meet Road 362 and the Little Lake-Sherwood Trail.

OPTION 2 turns left for a tangential ride on the narrow single track descending northwest. It drops for 2.5 miles via alternating single and double track to the North Fork Noyo River. See Ride #16 for details.

From Jackass Pass, **OPTION 1** turns right and descends steeply through dense forest on Road 362's rough tread. The descent eases by 4.3 miles, then Road 362 ends at 4.5 miles at Road 360.

OPTION 3 turns left on Road 360 to make the 6.3-mile loop described from this junction in Ride #25.) Option 1 turns right and descends gradually on uneven tread. After a concrete ford of Brandon Gulch, pass a yellow gate at 5.1 miles, then two boulders blocking the road. Come to the junction of Roads 360 and 361.

OPTION 4 turns left on Road 361. You can ride the easy, almost level 5.2-mile round trip to road's end (Ride #26, Option 1), or make the strenuous 8.9-mile loop, as described in Ride #26, Option 3.

Option 1 makes a sharp right turn and continues on Road 360. Make one short moderate climb to 5.5 miles, then descend past a yellow gate (generally locked in winter) and contour down the canyon of North Fork of the South Fork Noyo River past several campsites. When you reach Road 300 at 6.3 miles, turn right and cross the wooden bridge, returning to your starting point at 6.4 miles.

25

Brandon Gulch/Riley Ridge Loop

Jackson State Forest Roads 360, 1000 & 362, with options on Roads 361, 380 & 1000 East

This pleasant loop starts with an easy ascent of lovely Brandon Gulch, then climbs vigorously to the ridgetop, where you roller coaster to the northernmost corner of the state forest and beyond. Choose from Options 1 or 3 for short or long loops dropping back to your starting point. Other options are abundant, making this an ideal place to camp and explore in different directions for several days. The peaceful bike-in Camp 6, 1.4 miles from the starting point, is one of several great campsites in the area.

DIRECTIONS TO STARTING POINT: Turn east off Highway One onto Highway 20 at M.59.8, just south of Fort Bragg. Go 5.9 miles, then left on Road 350. In .3 mile, take the right fork. In 3 miles from the highway, pass the Camp One area. At 3.2 miles you come to a big intersection. Take Road 360 heading north. At 4.4 miles, just after crossing a bridge, park at the intersection of Roads 360 and 361. (In winter a gate at 4.1 miles is sometimes locked. If so, park there — do not block gate — and add .3 mile to distance.)

ELEVATION AT START: 140 feet

OPTION 1: Roads 360, 1000 and 362.
Moderate 7.7-mile loop, little or no vehicle traffic.
Elevation Gain/Loss: 1150 feet+/1150 feet-

OPTION 2: Roads 360, 1000, 380 and 360.
Moderate 11.4-mile loop, little or no vehicle traffic.
Elevation Gain/Loss: 1660 feet+/1660 feet-

OPTION 3: Add Road 1000 east.
Strenuous, add up to 26 miles, little or no vehicle traffic.
Elevation Gain/Loss: Add 2080 feet+/2080 feet- round trip to Road 200, about 12 miles

OPTION 4: Add Road 361 to any of above.

Easy, add 5.2 miles round trip, little or no vehicle traffic.

Elevation Gain/Loss: Add 90 feet+/90 feet-

SURFACE: Dirt logging roads

FACILITIES: Free camping in Camp One area, permit required, bring your own water. One possibility is Camp 6, 1.4 miles up Road 360 from the starting point, accessible only by walking or biking in.

MAP: Page 62

Ride Notes

The road you want to follow from the confusing 360/361 intersection heads northwest, then north up Brandon Gulch. If you are on the right road, you'll pass boulders, then a yellow gate. After a cement creek crossing, ascend gradually on rough tread following the gulch upstream.

At .7 mile Road 362 forks left — that's where Option 1 returns. Stay right on Road 360 and continue up the pretty gulch on an easy ascent. After the camp at 1.4 miles, your ascent soon turns moderate, then steep along a stretch cut by numerous deep water bars. While anyone but buff riders may have to walk this stretch, the worst of the hill is mercifully short.

The worst climbing has passed when you reach a junction at 2.2 miles. (Road 363 goes right for a quick descent to the starting point.) Bear left on ridgetop Road 360. The ascent continues in sporadic fashion, sometimes easy, sometimes steep, interspersed with a few short descents all the way to the end of Road 360 at 3.4 miles. There you meet Road 1000 atop Riley Ridge.

OPTION 3 turns right on Road 1000 to roller coaster on Riley Ridge and virtually the entire northern boundary of Jackson State Forest. You can ride Road 1000 to your heart's content — it ends at Highway 20 at the top of Seven Mile Grade after about 15 miles, but the last 2 miles are private property. Road 1000 is an open ended option limited only by your endurance and remaining daylight.

To continue **OPTION 1**, turn left on Road 1000, following Riley Ridge west and northwest. Like most ridgetop routes, you roller coaster up and down for the next 2.5 miles. These ups-and-downs are short, with little net change in elevation until 4.7 miles. Then you descend moderately and steeply to 5.3 miles to be rewarded with grand views north and west all the way to the Pacific. The long descent is followed by a steep .25-mile uphill, then more short roller-coaster runs to 6.3 miles, where you meet Road 362 at a ridgetop saddle called Jackass Pass.

The road numbers at this junction are unmarked, but on a redwood beside the junction on the left is a tattered hiker/horse symbol that designates the Little Lake-Sherwood (LLS) Trail. Road 362 on the left is the LLS Trail and the route back to the starting point. On the right (north) side of Road 1000, the LLS Trail descends northwest across private property. The narrow single track might look inviting, but you wouldn't want to run into a hiker or horse while barreling down the narrow track. If you take it, go slow! The sign on the single track says it's 2 miles to Noyo River, but it's 2.5 — see Ride #16.

OPTION 2 extends your ride on Road 1000, which climbs steeply south and west along the ridgetop. Return down Road 380 and up Road 360 to your starting point (see Ride #24).

Our Option 1 ride turns left on Road 362 to descend into a deep dark wooded canyon. Sit back, keep your head up and watch for rough spots as 362 descends steeply on occasional loose tread. The steep rough descent ends before Road 362's end at Road 360 at 7 miles. Turn right on 360 and make the short gradual descent to return to your starting point at 7.7 miles.

OPTION 4: When you return to the starting point and want to ride more, consider an easy cool-down ride heading east on level Road 361. It follows the North Fork of South Fork Noyo River for 2.6 miles before ending. At the east end is the start of the Trestle Trail, closed to cyclists because of steep up-and-down pitches with wooden steps crowded by poison oak. It offers a vigorous walk, up to 8.25 miles round trip.

If you're still not pooped and want some challenging single track, backtrack .5 mile on Road 361. There, near Camp 8, the Bob Woods Trail crosses the little river and ascends steeply east and south for 1.2 miles, ending at Road 330 (see Ride #26). Otherwise, backtrack west on Road 361 to your starting point.

26

North Fork of South Fork Noyo River & Ridge Loop

Road 361, with options on Bob Woods Trail & Roads 330, 332, 300 & 360

This is the Jekyll and Hyde of dirt rides, with several miles of easy, mostly level double track on Roads 361, 360 and 300 playing charming Dr. Jekyll. The churlish Mr. Hyde is played by Road 332/330's 1000-foot ascent in 3 miles, with a deserving stand-in by the lovely but unforgiving Bob Woods Trail (single track). Do what you want with this ride: remain in polite society on the level double track, or become a hill-devouring animal on the steep stuff. As you're descending the tight turns on Bob Woods Trail, just remember you may not be the only person rounding that blind corner. Other rides abound in this corner of Jackson State Forest.

DIRECTIONS TO STARTING POINT: Same as Ride #25.

ELEVATION AT START: 140 feet

OPTION 1: Road 361 to end.
Easy, 5.2 miles round trip, little or no vehicle traffic.
Elevation Gain/Loss: 90 feet+/90 feet-

OPTION 2: Road 361, Bob Woods Trail to top and return.
Advanced/Strenuous, 6.8 miles round trip, little or no vehicle traffic.
Elevation Gain/Loss: 990 feet+/990 feet-

OPTION 3: Road 361, Bob Woods Trail, Roads 330, 332, 300 and 360 loop.
Advanced/Strenuous, 9.1-mile loop, little or no vehicle traffic.
Elevation Gain/Loss: 1230 feet+/1230 feet-

SURFACE: Dirt roads, with single track option.

FACILITIES: Pit toilets and campsites on Road 361.

MAP: Page 62

Ride Notes

Head east on level Road 361, following the North Fork of South Fork Noyo River along its north bank. After a short rise and drop around .2 mile, contour east through forest along the meandering stream. Poison Oak Camp at .8 mile is much prettier than its name, but that bane of western explorers grows there. Pass a narrow spot on the road, then Camp Four at 1.4 miles. Ascend gently up the narrow river past 2.1 miles, where a sign on the right points south across the river for the Bob Woods Trail, a steep, challenging single track described in Option 2. Pass Camp Eight just beyond the spur and continue up Road 361 to its end at 2.6 miles. There you might consider a walk, but not a ride, up the Trestle Trail, which continues up this fork of the river nearly to its headwaters. Please respect the bike closure; the trail has many wooden steps and much poison oak. Easy Option 1 returns down Road 361 to your starting point.

OPTION 2: Only advanced, fit riders really want to consider riding up the Bob Woods Trail, one of the steepest, most challenging single tracks in the book. It's easier, but still difficult, to descend Bob Woods Trail as described in Option 3. But if you want the "E" ticket of ascents and descents in a short 2.4 miles of riding, leave Road 361 at the signed Bob Woods Trail start, around 2.15 miles from the starting point. Follow the faint single track east through Camp Eight and ford the little river to find obvious tread that bends sharply left and ascends extremely steeply east up a ridge. The awesomely steep, narrow-track ascent eases around 2.4 miles, then rises fitfully but often steeply along the ridgetop until you enter Bob Woods Opening at 2.7 miles. Ascend gradually, then moderately through the meadow. Please walk your bike when track is muddy. Before 3 miles, leave the top of the clearing and ascend a gully through the forest. Climb out of one gully by 3.1 miles and drop into a second gully, cross it and ascend steeply. By 3.3 miles your track becomes vague in rolling country with lots of blowdown. Follow the track south, ascending the left side of the gulch to a saddle on Road 330 on the ridgetop at 3.4 miles. Turn around and ride back down.

OPTION 3: To descend the Bob Woods Trail without climbing 900 feet in 1.2 miles takes a long loop, but it's a good one for skilled riders. Ride south on Road 360 from the starting point, retracing the route you just drove until the Road 300 junction at 1.2 miles. Turn left and follow Road 300 southeast to a locked gate at 1.6 miles, then continue a gentle ascent along the South Fork Noyo River to 2.4 miles, then turn left and ascend unmarked Road 332. Climb moderately and steeply past two spur roads to 2.9 miles. Then ascend gradually and moderately over water bars.

Your track contours before coming to a junction at 3.4 miles. Road 332 ends here. You want to turn left on Road 330, ascending moderately along a ridge. After passing a yellow gate at 4 miles, ascend steeply on occasionally rough tread. Your climb turns moderate around 4.4 miles, passing dead-end Road 334 on the left at 4.8 miles. Ascend gradually to the summit before 5 miles, then descend gradually and moderately to a saddle at 5.4 miles. Climb slightly and contour to another saddle at 5.6 miles.

Around the second saddle a recent logging operation has made a mess of the area around the upper Bob Woods trailhead. Where the road splits in two, take the left fork along the ridgetop. After a slight rise, another saddle around 5.7 miles is where the Woods Trail starts and descends north. Slash hides the track, but it leaves from the east side of a circle of redwoods, the largest of which is four feet in diameter and leans. (Road 330 continues east along the ridgetop through pretty country, never dropping below 1000 feet. Indian Springs Camp [permit required] is 2.7 miles east, road's end at Road 1000 is 5.7 miles.)

Descend north and northeast on Bob Woods Trail to find better track in 150 to 200 feet. You might have to carry your bike through here. Then descend on better tread, dropping steeply through a gulch. Top a short rise around 6 miles and drop into another gulch, following it into Bob Woods Opening by 6.2 miles. Your track turns west on an easy descent through the meadow to 6.4 miles, rises briefly, then begins its drop into the deep canyon below. Navigate the steepest, most hazardous descent from 6.7 miles to the bottom at 6.9 miles. Turn sharply right and ford the North Fork of South Fork Noyo River, passing Camp Eight and coming to Road 361. Turn left and cruise down the nearly level road, returning to your starting point at 9.1 miles.

27

South Slope of Hare Creek Headwaters

Jackson State Forest Road 450 east end, with options on Roads 456, 455, 508 & 500

These fun, easy loops offer balanced workouts. Unlike so many Jackson State Forest rides, here you'll find numerous short ups and downs spread over the loop instead of one long descent offset by a long climb. Options 1 and 3 have vigorous .5-mile ascents at their midpoints. The big uphill in the middle of Option 2 is longer but less steep. These double-track loops offer little technical challenge, just good exercise and back road boogie.

DIRECTIONS TO STARTING POINT: Turn east off Highway One at M.59.8 onto Highway 20. Go 8.1 miles, then turn right on unmarked Road 500. Just uphill, Road 450 is on your right behind a yellow gate. There's a wide spot on the left side of Road 500 ideal for parking. Don't block gate or Road 500.

ELEVATION AT START: 960 feet

OPTION 1: Roads 450, 456 and 500.
Easy, 6.6-mile loop, light vehicle traffic.
Elevation Gain/Loss: 800 feet+/800 feet-

OPTION 2: Roads 450, 455, 508 and 500.
Easy, 10.7-mile loop, light vehicle traffic.
Elevation Gain/Loss: 990 feet+/990 feet-

OPTION 3: Roads 450, 512, 510 and 500.
Moderate, 14.7-mile loop, light vehicle traffic.
Elevation Gain/Loss: 1610 feet+/1610 feet-

OPTION 4: Return via Roads 508 and/or 408 (steeper, shorter choices).
Moderate, light vehicle traffic.
Elevation Gain/Loss: Add 200 feet+/200 feet-

SURFACE: Mostly dirt state forest roads, pavement on Road 500.

MAP: Page 70

Ride Notes

Road 450 descends fitfully on good tread for the first 1.2 miles, broken by three short climbs. Descend unevenly for the next mile. Then two short ups and downs bring you to the signed junction with Road 456 at 2.75 miles. To complete Option 1, turn left and climb moderately .65 mile to paved Road 500, then turn left and make the easy climb along 500 until you drop to your starting point at 6.6 miles.

OPTION 2: For a longer loop, continue on Road 450 beyond Road 456. Watch for water bars and rougher tread on this leg as you descend unevenly to 4 miles, interrupted by two short climbs. The next 2 miles to the Road 455 junction at 6 miles consist of nine short ups and downs with no net change in elevation, a good workout without much difficulty. Ascend to the signed junction, turn left and climb moderately on Road 455's heavily water-barred ridge route, topping out where Road 455 ends at Road 508 at 6.9 miles. Turn left and descend Road 508 to its east end at 7.5 miles. Go left, following mostly paved but chuckholed Road 500 as it contours east. Stay on the paved surface at each junction (unless you choose Road 408, Option 4) After a bit of easy up and down, descend quickly to your starting point at 10.7 miles.

OPTION 3: Continue on Road 450 beyond Road 455, winding through pretty tributaries of Hare Creek on easy ups and downs to the unmarked junction with Road 512 at 8.5 miles. Turn left and ascend moderately to road's end at 9 miles, where you link with Ride #19, Option 3. Turn left and follow Road 510 briefly until it ends at Road 500. Turn left and follow paved Road 500 on its easy grade along the ridge dividing the watersheds of Hare Creek and Caspar Creek. Watch for traffic on this primary back road through the state forest. Return to your starting point at 14.7 miles.

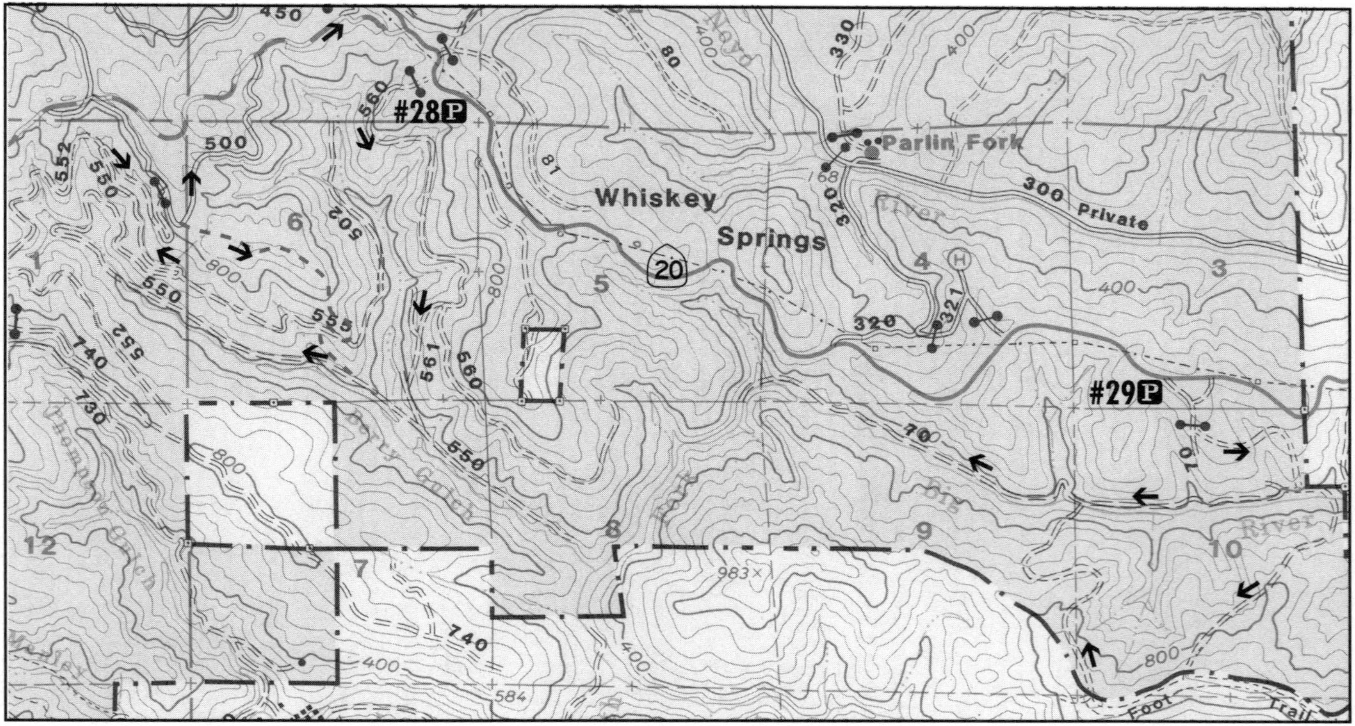
#28P
#29P
Whiskey Springs
Parlin Fork
20
300 Private
Foot Trail
River
983×

28

Berry Gulch

Roads 560, 561, 550, 500 & 408, with options on Roads 550 & 552 & single track

This loop offers an easy ride despite its elevation change. You'll see plenty of cutover forest, but the middle section follows a pretty canyon along Berry Gulch, a tributary of Little North Fork Big River.

The loop starts with a long descent into Berry Gulch, where you encounter a tiny stream tumbling over moss- and fern-draped rock shelves, a pretty spot for a break. A long gradual ascent follows the gulch almost to its head-waters. A well graded climb out of the gulch gains the ridge at paved Road 500. Contour along Road 500, then descend Road 408 briefly, finishing with a .3 mile-run up Highway 20. Options 2 and 3 add spur roads to this basic loop, while Option 4 offers a second loop: a steep, challenging single-track descent back to the bottom of Berry Gulch, and a repeat of the climb out.

DIRECTIONS TO STARTING POINT: Turn east off Highway One at M.59.8 onto Highway 20. Go 8.7 miles to a big south bend where unmarked Road 560 descends behind a yellow gate. Do not block gate when you park.

ELEVATION AT START: 950 feet

OPTION 1: Roads 560, 561, 550, 500, 408 and Highway 20.
Easy, 7.9-mile loop, little or no vehicle traffic (except highway).
Elevation Gain/Loss: 740 feet+/740 feet-

OPTION 2: Add east end of Road 550.
Easy, add 1 mile round trip.
Elevation Gain/Loss: Add 120 feet+/120 feet-

OPTION 3: Add Road 552.
Moderate, add 3 miles round trip.
Elevation Gain/Loss: Add 840 feet+/840 feet-

OPTION 4: Add second loop — steep skid trail descent and repeat climb out.
Advanced, add 5.1-mile loop.
Elevation Gain/Loss: Add 710 feet+/710 feet-

SURFACE: Dirt forest roads (except Road 500 and highway — paved — and single track on Option 4).

Ride Notes

An almost continuous descent on double-track Roads 560 and 561 is broken by two very short climbs. The tread is generally good, with rough spots and water bars after 1 mile. Scotch broom crowds the road's lower end, making it single track in spots. After one last deep water bar at 2.1 miles, Road 561 ends at Road 550. (You can add an easy mile by going left on dead-end Road 550 — **OPTION 2.**)

Turn right on 550 and pass the bottom of Option 4's single track, then enjoy the long gradual ascent up the pretty creek and canyon. The road crosses the creek twice around 3.6 miles, then switchbacks to the right at the head of the gulch and begins a steady climb out of the canyon.

At 4.5 miles, veer left on more traveled Road 550 — Road 555 on your right is overgrown. At 5.2 miles, Road 550 comes to a T intersection. On the left is dead-end Road 552. (Add up to 3 miles by going left to the end of 552 and back — **OPTION 3.**) To complete the loop, turn right on Road 550 and ascend gradually.

Pass a yellow gate at 5.8 miles; Road 550 ends at broad Road 500. Turn right and follow 500's mostly paved, often uneven tread on a gentle ascent, watching and listening for motorized traffic. In just .1 mile, the unmarked road on the right is Option 4. Road 500 climbs gently, merging with Road 408 at 7.1 miles. At 7.3 miles, turn right on gravel Road 408 for a short drop to Highway 20 at 7.6 miles. Turn right and ascend gradually on Highway 20's shoulder to complete a 7.9-mile loop.

OPTION 4: For a challenging single-track descent, turn right at 5.9 miles and ascend the double track east along a ridgetop. Where the road forks, go right and quickly come to a top, then descend moderately along the edge of a clearcut on bumpy track cut by water bars. After a flat spot at .5 mile, descend steeply on single track. Leave the clearcut at .7 mile and drop very steeply along the ridgetop, with a very rough section around .85 mile. The steep drop continues through big bends on slippery tread, leveling at Road 555 at 1 mile. Go right on 555 briefly, then go left on better tread single track, dropping steeply, then moderately. After a short rise at 1.2 miles, plunge steeply on rutted tread to the track's end at Road 550 at 1.35 miles. Turn right and repeat the ascent out of Berry Gulch.

29

Headwaters of Little North Fork Big River

Jackson State Forest Road 70

This ride descends to the headwaters of Little North Fork Big River and explores three miles along the stream. The only option climbs to a ridge south of the watershed, then drops back down, offering a more arduous, but still short workout.

DIRECTIONS TO STARTING POINT: Turn east off Highway One south of Fort Bragg at M.59.8 onto Highway 20. Go 11.9 miles to a south bend where unmarked Road 70 is behind a yellow gate. Do not block gate when you park.

ELEVATION AT START: 720 feet

OPTION 1: Road 70.
　　　　　Easy, 5.8 miles round trip, no vehicle traffic.
　　　　　Elevation Gain/Loss: 480 feet+/480 feet-

OPTION 2: Road 70 — spur to ridge.
　　　　　Moderate, 6.5-mile loop, no vehicle traffic.
　　　　　Elevation Gain/Loss: 930 feet+/930 feet-

OPTION 3: Options 1 and 2 combined.
　　　　　Moderate, 8.5-mile semi-loop, no vehicle traffic.
　　　　　Elevation Gain/Loss: 1000 feet+/1000 feet-

SURFACE: Dirt forest roads

MAP: Page 98

Ride Notes

Behind the yellow gate, Road 70 contours. At .1 mile turn right and descend behind another yellow gate. Descend moderately on good tread

101

with well packed water bars.

At .9 mile is an important junction where Option 2 (described below) goes left. Easy Option 1 (Road 70) turns right and descends gradually on good tread, following the north bank of Little North Fork Big River. It passes some large redwoods in an area that was extensively logged. Your easy descent follows excellent tread until another junction at 1.9 miles. Beyond the junction, the tread is little traveled, overgrown in places with young conifers. When the tread becomes rough and rocky at the base of a cutbank, you're approaching the end of Road 70. At 2.9 miles it is washed out at the crossing of a rust colored creek. While the tread continues beyond the creek, the road's true end is not far beyond. Turn back, making the easy climb back to the first junction, then the moderate ascent back to Highway 20.

OPTION 2: Go left at the .9-mile junction and descend across the headwaters of Little North Fork Big River at 1 mile, then climb moderately on uneven tread. Ignore the numerous spur roads — logging skid trails that quickly dead-end. At 2.2 miles you pass a gate. Gain the ridgetop at 2.3 miles, where a road forks left to head east. Shown on the map as a "Foot Trail," it follows the state forest boundary about .5 mile to private property. Stay right at the junction and head west, contouring along a brushy ridgetop.

At another fork at 2.6 miles, both roads leave the ridgetop. Go right to stay on state forest property. Contour to 2.8 miles, then make a fun, winding descent (but watch the water bars!). Stay on the main track and the road crosses the "river" and ends at 4.4 miles. For the shorter loop turn right and climb gradually to the headwaters junction, then moderately to your starting point.

OPTION 3: Extend Option 2 by turning left on Road 70 and riding 1 mile to road's end. Return up Road 70 to your starting point.

30

Chamberlain Creek Watershed

Jackson State Forest Roads 230, 231 & 202, with options on Roads 1000, 250, 200, 240 & 330

The Chamberlain Creek area offers a maze of options, only a few of which we detail here. This tributary of North Fork Big River collects the waters of most of the eastern half of the state forest. The first three options start with a vigorous ascent on Road 230, a little traveled route along the watershed's eastern edge.

Option 4 offers a special treat — visit one of the forest's prettiest places, the Chamberlain Creek Waterfall. You'll need to park your bike and walk the final steep, stepped ¼ mile, but it's worth it. For an easy ride with slightly more traffic, do Option 4 from the starting point.

DIRECTIONS TO STARTING POINT: Turn east off Highway One at M.59.8 onto Highway 20. Go east to M.17.35, just past the Chamberlain Creek bridge, then turn left on dirt Road 200. Go .5 mile to Road 230 on the right. Park near the junction.

ELEVATION AT START: 390 feet

OPTION 1: Roads 230, 231 and 202.
Moderate, 4.5-mile loop, little or no vehicle traffic.
Elevation Gain/Loss: 960 feet+/960 feet-

OPTION 2: Roads 230, 1000, 250 and 200.
Moderate, 12.5-mile loop, little or no vehicle traffic.
Elevation Gain/Loss: 1870 feet+/1870 feet-

OPTION 3: Roads 230, 1000, 240 and 200.
Strenuous, 14.2-mile loop, little or no vehicle traffic.
Elevation Gain/Loss: 2400 feet+/2400 feet-

OPTION 4: Add Road 200 to Waterfall Trail, Roads 200 and 330 to Indian Springs Camp.
Easy, add 7 miles round trip to trail, or moderate, 15 miles round

103

trip to camp, little or no vehicle traffic.

Elevation Gain/Loss: Add 480 feet+/480 feet- to trail, 1980 feet+/ 1980 feet- to camp.

SURFACE: Dirt forest roads

FACILITIES: Camp 20 Recreation Area, where you leave Highway 20, has phone, picnic area and pit toilets. Free camping at Dunlap Camp .7 mile west. Remote Camp at Indian Springs, Option 4.

Ride #30

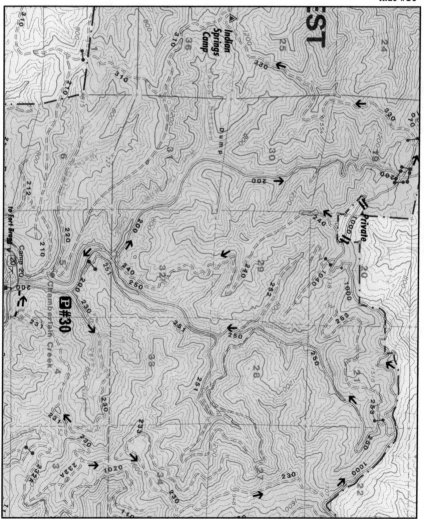

Ride Notes

Follow Road 230 east on a gradual incline up Park Gulch. At .4 mile the ascent eases along the pleasant creek canyon. You soon begin a long moderate ascent. Around .8 mile the forest thins for views of the high ridges around you. The winding ascent continues to a junction at 2 miles.

OPTION 1 forks right on signed Road 231. Ascending southwest on uneven tread, it quickly comes to a 1200-foot summit. Roller coaster west along the ridgetop to 2.8 miles, then descend steeply on rough tread. Drop by big bends left and right into a wooded gulch. Where the road forks before 3.7 miles, turn right on unmarked Road 202 and descend and contour to Road 200. Turn right and ride .4 mile to the starting point.

OPTIONS 2 & 3: Turn left at the 2-mile junction and ascend on Road 230. Breaks in the forest on your right offer views over the canyons of North Fork Big River. By 2.1 miles the climb turns moderate, sometimes steep. After big bends right and left, pass Road 232A on the right at 2.75 miles. Continue up the ridge on Road 230. After a dip at 2.9 miles, ascend steeply on rutted tread, then moderately past Road 233 on the left. A short gradual descent ends at 3.5 miles. Ascend moderately on the ridgetop, dip briefly around 3.8 miles, then climb steeply with grand views south over much of the Big River watershed. Descend to a saddle at 4.3 miles, then rise and drop fitfully. After a spur on the left at 4.7 miles, ascend to a top at 4.8 miles. Road 230 continues roller coastering along the ridgetop over five more knobs. The last top at 5.4 miles is the ride's 1950-foot summit. Descend moderately to Road 230's end at 5.95 miles.

Turn left on broad ridgetop Road 1000, descending to 6.4 miles, then contouring with views north over the Noyo watershed. Descend to a junction at 7 miles.

OPTION 2 turns left to descend Road 250. Drop moderately through four big bends. At the fourth bend at 7.6 miles, Road 253 forks right. (You can take a side trip on Road 253's rough tread through the headwaters of Chamberlain Creek — I followed it 4.6 miles to find no exit — a very steep hill at 1.2 miles discourages further progress.) Continue the moderate descent on Road 250 through sweeping curves. Beyond 8 miles, cross Chamberlain Creek three times, then descend gradually with the creek on your right. Several tributaries join the main creek in its rocky canyon. Ascend briefly before 10 miles, passing the upper end of spur Road 251 on the left.

Descend gradually along the pretty canyon, passing the bottom end of Road 240 on the right at 11.6 miles. Merge with Road 200 at 11.7 miles (where Option 4 turns right) and continue down canyon, returning to your starting point at 12.5 miles.

OPTION 3 continues west on Road 1000 at the 7-mile junction. Ascend fitfully, with one dip, to 7.9 miles. Contour, then descend to a saddle at 9 miles. Ascend Road 1000 on big bends left and right, then pass Road 1040 on the left. Contour along the ridgetop to the next road that forks left around 9.6 miles. Road 1000 continues onto private property, so turn left on Road 240, Center Ridge Road. Road 240 makes a steep ascent with one dip, coming to its 1620-foot summit at 10 miles. Soon you descend southeast, then roller coaster along the ridgetop to 10.8 miles. Road 240 follows the ridgetop on a steep descent on orange-clay tread that's very slippery when wet. Watch for deep water bars. After a big bend right, wind through a wooded gulch, then descend fitfully, with grand views down Chamberlain Creek to the North Fork Big River watershed. Your descent turns steep around 12.7 miles, passing two more deep water bars and dropping steeply by rough tread. Road 240 ends at Road 250 at 13.3 miles. Turn right and follow 250 briefly until it merges with Road 200 (see Option 4). It is .8 mile down Road 200 to the starting point.

OPTION 4: Ascend Road 200, from either the Road 250 junction or the starting point. The dirt double track ascends gradually along the canyon of West Chamberlain Creek. About 2 miles from Road 250, the ascent turns moderate and winding. At 3.5 miles look for a wide shoulder on the left, where a wooden railing marks the steep footpath. Lock your bike and walk the ¼ mile to the base of the falls.

To continue to Indian Springs Camp, ascend north on Road 200 to its four-corners junction with Road 1000 at 4 miles. Turn left and follow Road 1000 about .25 mile to the first fork. Go left on Road 330, ascending steeply to a ridgetop knob around 4.7 miles. Road 330 dips and rises twice to its 1554-foot summit before 6 miles. Descend then contour along the ridge. Indian Springs Camp is on the right at 7.5 miles. You need a permit to camp. Road 330 continues northwest on a pleasant ridgetop run, connecting with Ride #26 at the top of the Bob Woods Trail in 2.7 miles.

31

North Fork Big River from Chamberlain Creek

Jackson State Forest Roads 800, 830, 920 & 810, with options on Roads 930 & 900

This pleasant loop begins with an easy ascent on pavement, then climbs moderately on narrow double track to gain a ridgetop, then follow it, with views extending for miles. After some roller-coaster runs and a few short steep climbs, the ridgetop route descends to a junction. From there you can extend your ride along the ridgetop (Option 2) or take a fun, easy route back, dropping down a winding double track, then going left along a broad road beside the wooded, meandering North Fork Big River.

DIRECTIONS TO STARTING POINT: Turn east off Highway One at M.59.8 onto Highway 20. Go east to M.17.5, just past the Chamberlain Creek bridge, then turn right on the paved road and park on the right. This is Road 800.

ELEVATION AT START: 300 feet

OPTION 1: Roads 800, 830, 920 and 810.
Moderate, 10.8-mile loop, little or no vehicle traffic.
Elevation Gain/Loss: 1610 feet+/1610 feet-

OPTION 2: Roads 800, 830, 920, 930, 900 and 810.
Strenuous, 12.3-mile loop, little or no vehicle traffic.
Elevation Gain/Loss: 2170 feet+/2170 feet-

OPTION 3: Add east end of 930 and 920 to Option 2.
Strenuous, 13.6-mile loop, little or no vehicle traffic.
Elevation Gain/Loss: 2490 feet+/2490 feet-

OPTION 4: Add full length of Road 900 to one of first 3 options. See Ride #32.
Moderate to strenuous, 20- or 21-mile loop or double loop.
Elevation Gain/Loss: 2980 feet+/- or 3660 feet+/-

SURFACE: Mostly dirt forest roads.

FACILITIES: Phone, picnic area, pit toilets at Camp 20 Recreation Area just west of Chamberlain Creek. Free camping at Dunlap Camp .7 mile west, or at Horse Camp on route, permit required.

MAP: Page 110

Ride Notes

Follow the paved road away from the highway, going right at the first junction (you'll return via the left fork). The paved road climbs gently, then descends gently as the surface becomes rougher. Contour to an important junction at 1.7 miles. Road 800 continues onto private property (signed no trespassing). Turn left on the narrow dirt double track of unsigned Road 830, ascending moderately, then gradually. At 2.4 miles, take the right fork (left fork dead-ends), crossing the seasonal creek you've been following, then climbing moderately.

You soon gain a ridge, then climb fitfully. The mostly moderate ascent gains a knob on the ridgetop at 3.9 miles. After a short moderate descent, roller coaster along the ridgetop. Reach a second top at 4.2 miles where a spur on the right heads south onto private property. Stay left and follow the ridgetop with grand views south and a few vistas north, following the state forest boundary. A long descent of increasing pitch gives way to a steep climb to 4.7 miles. Then it's down and up again to Option 1's highest point (1200 feet) at 5.5 miles.

Watch for water bars as you drop moderately, then climb once more before leaving the ridgetop to descend to an unmarked junction at 6.1 miles. Road 830 ends here at Road 920. Option 2 turns right to climb back to the ridgetop. Option 1 goes left, descending northwest on a pleasant twisting run on good tread. After some rough tread around 6.4 miles, good tread resumes for a gradual descent to a yellow gate at 6.9 miles.

At the four-way junction beyond the gate, Option 1 goes left on broad Road 810. The track straight ahead and the right fork are Road 900. (If you go straight you'll come to Highway 20 in .6 mile. **OPTION 4** takes the right fork if you want a longer ride — see Ride #32.) Go left for Option 1, contouring northwest on good surface. From 7.7 miles, Road 810 descends gradually to 8.2 miles, then climbs gradually for .5 mile, following the south bank of North Fork Big River. The down-up pattern repeats to 9.3 miles. Then descend gradually on partially paved broad track. At 9.5 miles a spur on the right enters a pleasant horse camp beside the placid river. Equestrians have priority to use the camp, but there's usually room for everyone, whether you want to picnic or stay overnight (permit required for camping).

Road 810 continues west. After an easy .5 mile ascent, make a short, easy descent to complete the loop and return to your starting point at 10.4 miles.

OPTION 2: If you turn right at the junction at 6.1 miles, ascend moderately, then steeply to gain a 1600-foot knob on the ridgetop before 7 miles. After a short descent, come to a junction with Road 930 around 7.2 miles. Road 920 continues along the ridgetop, but our described loop makes a sharp left to descend steeply on Road 930 to its end at Road 900 at 8.2 miles. Go left again and descend to the next junction at 8.8 miles, where Road 900 turns right to drop to Highway 20. The nicest way back is to go straight at the junction, following Road 810 back to your starting point for a 12.3-mile loop.

OPTION 3: Follow Option 2 to the junction around 7.2 miles and stay right instead of going left. Road 920 climbs over a ridgetop knob and descends to another junction with Road 930. Go left and follow 930 as it descends steeply, then climbs gradually back to the ridgetop. At the junction there you can go left and retrace your tracks on Road 920 along the ridgetop, then descend Road 920 to the four-way intersection; or you can turn right and descend steeply on Road 930 to Road 900, where you go left to the four-way intersection. Either way, head west on Road 810 from the intersection to return to your starting point.

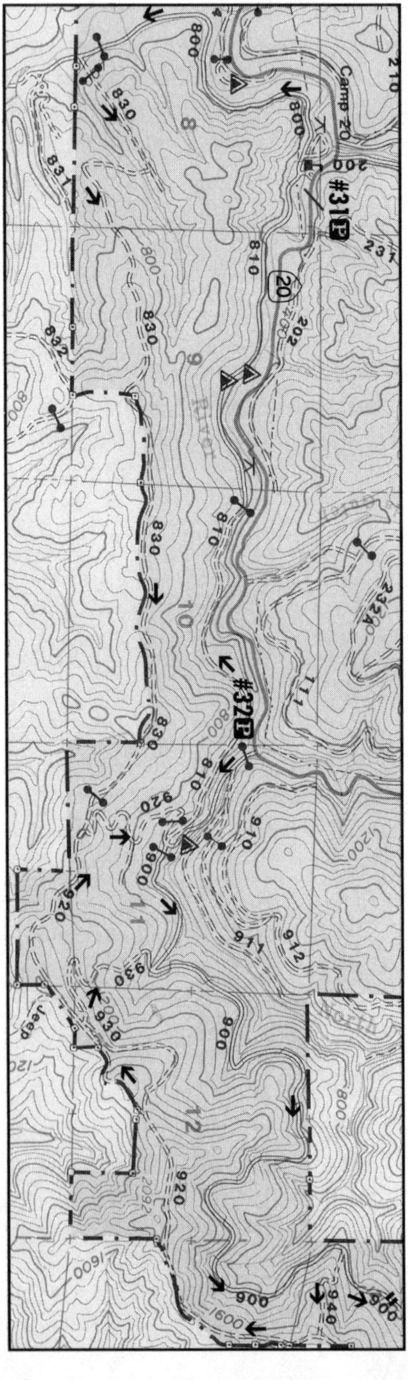
#31
#32
Camp 20
20
River
Jeep

32

Headwaters of North Fork Big River

Jackson State Forest Road 900, with options on Roads 940, 920 & 930

This ride starts out easy, turns to a moderately challenging ascent, then makes a gentle winding descent to the easternmost corner of Jackson State Forest. Option 1 returns by the same track for an easy second half. Options 2 and 3 offer considerably more challenging routes of both physical and technical challenge. They ascend steeply to a 2092-foot hilltop, then plunge wildly on primitive track, one of the most challenging descents in the book, 1300 feet in 2 miles. The descent's final leg picks up good double track, finishing easy by retracing your starting track. You can link with Ride #31, either on the ridge or down below to expand this into an exciting, diverse 22-mile ride.

DIRECTIONS TO STARTING POINT: Turn east off Highway One at M.59.8, onto Highway 20. Go east to M.20.0, just before the James Creek bridge. Turn right and park at the start of paved, unmarked Road 900.

WARNING!: This area can be very hot from May through September.

ELEVATION AT START: 470 feet

OPTION 1: Road 900 to end and return.
Moderate, 10.3 miles round trip, little or no vehicle traffic.
Elevation Gain/Loss: 1370 feet+/1370 feet-

OPTION 2: Roads 900, 940, 920 and 930.
Strenuous, 10.7-mile loop, little or no vehicle traffic.
Elevation Gain/Loss: 2050 feet+/2050 feet-

OPTION 3: Roads 900, 940, 920 and 900.
Strenuous, 10.9-mile loop, little or no vehicle traffic.
Elevation Gain/Loss: 2240 feet+/2240 feet-

OPTION 4: Add Ride #31 to one of choices above.
Strenuous, 21.5-mile (or more) loop, little or no vehicle traffic.

SURFACE: Dirt forest roads. Options 2 and 3 have single track.

FACILITIES: Free camping at Forks Camp, pit toilet, trash bin.

Ride Notes

Paved Road 900 dips across James Creek, then ascends gradually on deteriorating pavement, crossing the river and passing Forks Camp at .2 mile. Ascend to a four-way junction at .65 mile. Turn left on Road 900 behind a rusty yellow gate, ascending gradually to 1 mile, then moderately. A short drop ends at the unmarked junction with steep Road 930 on your right at 1.3 miles.

Pedal up Road 900, a gradual climb on some rough, rocky tread. Your ascent turns moderate from 1.5 to 1.8 miles. The tread improves as the hill becomes gradual. Ascend moderately from 2.1 miles, then steeply around 2.5 miles. Your ascent soon eases, with views over the canyon of North Fork Big River around 2.8 miles. The ascent turns steep around 3 miles on uneven, rocky tread. At 3.1 miles an unmapped fork descends left. Road 900 soon reverts to an easy climb, then twists through fun curves on short ups and downs.

By 3.4 miles, start a gradual descent with a view north to Sherwood Peak beyond Three Chop Ridge. The downhill has good tread, but watch for big rocks. The descent ends at 4.2 miles after playful dips and turns. Ascend an easy hill broken by a short dip.

A vague spur on the right at 4.65 miles is unmarked Road 940. Option 1 follows Road 900 on an easy descent to its end at 5.15 miles. Turn around and retrace your tracks on Road 900, ascending to the summit at 7.1 miles, followed by the long, almost all downhill run back to the starting point at 10.3 miles.

OPTION 2 turns right on the rough track of Road 940. At the start you can see your goal: the wooded ridge above. Road 940's steep, eroded start will probably force a dismount, but most of the road's .7 mile offers narrow, uneven but manageable tread. Fork right where the track splits .2 mile from Road 900.

By 6.4 miles Road 940 ends at the broad ridgetop track of Road 920. If you turn left at the junction, Road 920 runs about .5 mile to the easternmost point in Jackson State Forest, where it meets private property only a mile as the raven flies from the 2748-foot pinnacle called Two Rock. Our described ride turns right at the junction and descends to a saddle at 6.5 miles, then rises moderately following the ridgetop.

At 7.2 miles the road forks. Take the right fork, climbing moderately on the ridgetop's north face.

Reach one summit at 7.3 miles. The path narrows, overgrown by brush as it contours, then ascends to the highest point at 7.4 miles. A spur on the left climbs steeply to the top of this 2092-foot hill. Your descent starts moderately from the summit, but sit back and keep the brakes handy.

At 7.6 miles the bottom drops out. Descend steeply, with rough tread around 7.7 miles. When the track forks at 7.9 miles, stay left on the ridgetop for a short rise to another top. Then make the steepest descent of all until 8.2 miles, where the track levels suddenly at a junction.

Stay left and contour along the ridgetop until 8.4 miles, where Road 920 jogs sharply left and climbs. (**OPTION 3:** A left on 920 follows the ridgetop up-down-up about a mile to the junction with Road 830, at the 6.1-mile point on Ride #31, where you go right on 920.) This description turns right on unmarked Road 930 to descend gradually, then moderately through sweeping curves. Where the descent eases around 8.9 miles, watch out for a deep hole on the left. The mostly steep descent to Road 930's end is fun but treacherous — rough in places, with patches of loose gravel. Veer right as you pass a big landing at 9.3 miles, dropping steeply to Road 900 at 9.4 miles.

Turn left and descend Road 900, returning to the four-way junction at 10 miles. A right turn descends to your starting point by 10.7 miles.

OPTION 4: Combine any of the first three options with Ride #31 for a 21.5-mile or longer ride. To combine Ride #31 with Option 1 or 2 above, go west on Road 810 at the four-way intersection, or, for a more challenging ride, go south/southwest on Roads 920/830, following Ride #31 in reverse direction. To combine Ride #31 with Option 3 above, go left at the Road 920/830 junction and follow Ride #31 in reverse.

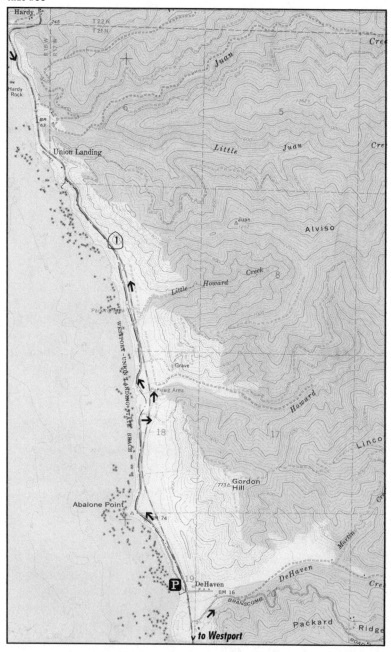

33

Westport-Union Landing State Beach

Park roads, with options on Highway One & Branscomb Road

Rocky 47-acre Westport-Union Landing State Beach sprawls along the rugged coast north of Westport. Here cyclists can ride about two miles of paved road with limited vehicle traffic, enjoying expansive views of the continent's dramatic western edge. This narrow shelf of coastal grasslands backed by steep hills is a favorite browsing area for deer. The tidal zone teems with marine life. The ride offers great whale watching in season (December to May) and a chance to walk the pink-streaked sands of Howard Creek Beach. The first two options are ideal for families with young children. More intrepid explorers can extend the ride, following the broad highway north to where it turns inland, or make an invigorating ascent on nearby Branscomb Road.

DIRECTIONS TO STARTING POINT: Turn west off Highway One at M.79.3, north of Westport. Park at the first lot.

ELEVATION AT START: 50 feet

OPTION 1: Park road north to Howard Creek.
Easy, 2.5 miles round trip, little or no vehicle traffic.
Elevation Gain/Loss: 70 feet+/70 feet-

OPTION 2: Park road north to Vista Point, short highway segment.
Easy, 4.1 miles round trip, little or no vehicle traffic, except highway — medium traffic.
Elevation Gain/Loss: 100 feet+/100 feet-

OPTION 3: Continue north on highway to Hardy Creek.
Easy, 8.1 miles round trip, medium vehicle traffic on highway.
Elevation Gain/Loss: 500 feet+/500 feet-

OPTION 4: Add a hill climb on nearby Branscomb Road.
Moderate, add 3.6 miles round trip, light to medium vehicle traffic.
Elevation Gain/Loss: Add 530 feet+/530 feet-

SURFACE: Paved

FACILITIES: Pit toilets, picnic area, phone, campground, water available must be purified.

Ride Notes

Ride north along the paved road on a gentle ascent overlooking the coast. Pass a seasonal campground loop around .1 mile, then watch for a hole in the pavement on the left that drops to the rocky tidal zone. Your road contours from .3 mile, heading toward Abalone Point past another campground loop, then a stairway to the beach on your left. Pass another hole in the road and come to Abalone Point around .7 mile.

Squeeze between posts that divert vehicles into the campground on your right and continue north on narrowing pavement along coastal bluffs, unimpeded by motor traffic. Beyond some willows crowding the pavement, descend slightly. Pass more posts at 1.1 miles and watch for vehicle traffic at another campground loop. Your road passes a path to Howard Creek Beach, veers right and ends at Highway One at 1.25 miles. Option 1 returns the way you came.

OPTION 2: To continue north you must ride the broad highway shoulder across the Howard Creek bridge. It offers a view of sheltered Howard Creek Ranch, a cozy B&B in a pioneer homestead. At 1.6 miles, carefully cross the highway and return to the park road. Turn right as the road forks and contour along the bluffs past more campsites. Reach the end of the campground and veer around a silver gate at 1.9 miles, coming to a vista point. You can continue about 800 feet to pavement's end at the mouth of Little Howard Creek. The site of the 1900-vintage lumber town called Union Landing is about a mile north. State Beach land extends nearly that far, but there is no path. Option 2 retraces your route to the starting point, 4.1 miles round trip.

OPTION 3: To continue north along this rugged shore, you must double back to the vista point entrance, then ride the highway shoulder on a gentle ascent. The road narrows through big curves. From 3 miles you descend slightly for .5 mile, passing the site of Union Landing west of the highway around 3.3 miles. Cross the Juan Creek bridge spanning the mouth of a big canyon, then ascend gradually with more grand coastal vistas. Just after topping a hill at 4 miles, the Shoreline Highway turns inland at Hardy Creek. Pause to absorb the coast's rugged grandeur before you turn back. Knife-edged Cape Vizcaino plunges to the surf two miles north, the Lost Coast hidden behind it. Many offshore rocks and sea stacks punctuate the shore. Needle-eyed Hardy Rock rises to the south. Eagles and puffins are sometimes seen along this jagged edge of the continent. Return along the ocean side of the highway. Back at the vista point, you can either ride the sleepy side roads again or continue along the highway. Either way you return to your starting point around 8.1 miles.

OPTION 4: If you want to end your outing with a vigorous hill climb, ride south .2 mile on the highway shoulder, then turn east on Branscomb Road. It is important to stay on the road's right shoulder — many blind curves ahead. Branscomb Road drops slightly to DeHaven Creek at .3 mile. Ascend moderately across a verdant hillside. The climb turns gradual around 1.2 miles. You soon come to Packard Ridge, passing homesteads before the pavement ends at 1.8 miles. To continue east involves steep ascents on rough tread, dusty in summer, muddy in winter. (The summit is 5 miles, at 1980 feet.) I recommend turning back here. To explore another paved portion of Branscomb Road, see Ride #34.

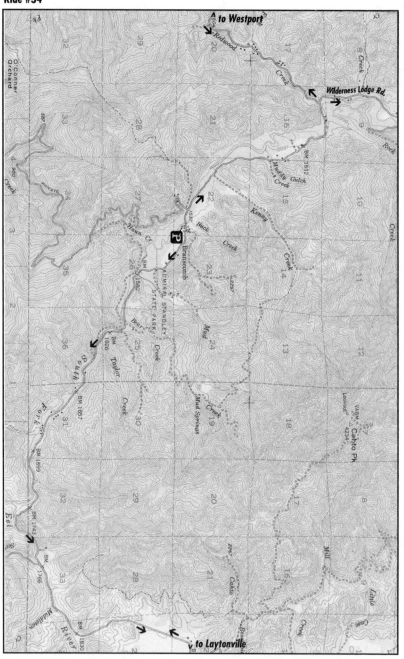

to Westport

Wilderness Lodge Rd.

to Laytonville

34

Branscomb Valley

Branscomb Road, with option on Wilderness Lodge Road

The remote Branscomb Valley offers gentle terrain in the heart of the Coast Range. Branscomb Road runs 26 miles from Coast Highway One to Laytonville on Highway 101. The westernmost 8 miles are steep and mostly unpaved, but virtually all the rest of this back road offers easy and excellent cycling opportunities. Branscomb Road has medium traffic, so it's important to ride single file on the road's right shoulder, especially on weekdays when logging trucks are often most of the traffic.

DIRECTIONS TO STARTING POINT: Turn onto Branscomb Road from Highway One at M.79.1, north of Westport, or from Highway 101 at M.70 in Laytonville. Drive to the Branscomb Store, 12.9 miles of dirt and paved road from the coast, 13 paved miles from Laytonville. Park across the road from the store, being careful to not block traffic in the sometimes busy parking area.

WARNING!: Branscomb can be hot in summer. Stay on road shoulder. Please respect private property and cycling ban at Northern California Coast Range Preserve.

ELEVATION AT START: 1540 feet

OPTION 1: Ride east on Branscomb Road through Admiral William Standley State Park and beyond.
Easy, 15.4 miles round trip, medium vehicle traffic.
Elevation Gain/Loss: 500 feet+/500 feet-

OPTION 2: Ride west toward the coast.
Easy, 10 miles round trip, medium vehicle traffic.
Elevation Gain/Loss: 190 feet+/190 feet-

OPTION 3: Add Wilderness Lodge Road to Option 2.
Easy, 7 miles round trip, light vehicle traffic.
Elevation Gain/Loss: Add 300 feet+/300 feet-

SURFACE: Paved county roads

FACILITIES: Branscomb Store has snacks, gas, phone.

Ride Notes

OPTION 1: Ride east from downtown Branscomb on the two-lane black-top of Branscomb Road. Traverse a large meadow in the bottom of a gentle valley rimmed by forest. You follow the South Fork Eel River (on your right) upstream toward its headwaters. The incline is gentle over-all, almost unnoticeable at first. By .7 mile the pavement narrows at tiny Admiral William Standley State Park, where a small but impressive grove of virgin redwood giants lines your route. Cross Mud Creek at 1 mile, its gray waters tinted by bubbling mud pots upstream (on private property).

Round a big bend left at 1.1 miles and leave the park for open coun-try, grasslands scattered with knots of conifers and oaks. Pass some giant stumps around 1.4 miles. If you envision the many stumps in this valley as giant trees, you'll have an inkling of the primeval forest here. Begin the most pronounced incline on this leg, a gradual ascent that gains 100 feet in 1.3 miles, 200 feet in 3 miles. Pass a few homesteads along the way.

Your ascent turns gentle again around 4.5 miles. By 5.3 miles you've left the remnant conifer forest for natural oak woodlands with large grassy clearings, a good area to spot hawks and golden eagles. The gentle incline continues to around 7 miles, where you turn north away from the river. Ascend gradually to the summit at 7.7 miles, where you look northeast into Long Valley 300 feet below. Option 1 turns back here. For a more challenging ride, it is 5.5 miles to Branscomb Road's end at Highway 101 in Laytonville.

OPTION 2: Head west from the Branscomb Store for a similarly easy ramble, mostly on two-lane pavement. This ride descends along the South Fork Eel River, but much of the descent is so slight you won't notice. Pass the Branscomb sawmill at .2 mile, one of the largest surviv-ing independent redwood mills. Beyond the mill, traffic decreases (es-pecially weekdays) as you parallel the river. Ascend slightly from .5 mile, angling away from the river to the north side of the narrow valley. Descend gently from 1.3 miles, passing several homesteads. Cross a bridge over the South Fork at 2.4 miles and continue with the river directly on your right. After crossing a bridge over Redwood Creek at its confluence with the South Fork at 3 miles, pass Wilderness Lodge Road on your right (see Option 3).

Branscomb Road turns southwest on a gentle ascent along Redwood Creek. A few remnant virgin redwoods tower over the young forest. Cross Redwood Creek again at 3.9 miles and continue up the gentle incline on broad pavement. A very wide spot in the road at 4.5 miles offers a place to park if you're doing a shuttle. At 5 miles the pavement ends, a good place to turn back.

If you continue on the rough dirt and gravel surface, use extreme caution and stay on the far right hand side of the road. Branscomb Road ascends 400 feet to a summit at 6.3 miles, then drops almost 2000 feet to end at Highway One 12.9 miles from Branscomb.

OPTION 3: Turn north off Branscomb Road onto Wilderness Lodge Road at M.9.8. This paved but narrow country lane follows the South Fork Eel River downstream on a gentle downhill past several homesteads. Cross Dutch Charlie Creek at .6 mile, then Little Charlie Creek at 1.1 miles. Cross to the right side of the South Fork at 1.7 miles, descending along the river to 2 miles. Then ascend gradually to 2.6 miles, winding away from the river. Drop back down near the river and enter the Northern California Coast Range Preserve around 3 miles. You can continue only to the preserve headquarters at 3.5 miles. This Nature Conservancy preserve is off limits to cyclists due to its sensitive habitats and abundant wildlife. Please respect this important restriction. The preserve is patrolled. You are welcome to lock your bike at headquarters and take a hike on the preserve's 7520 acres. Otherwise head back the way you came.

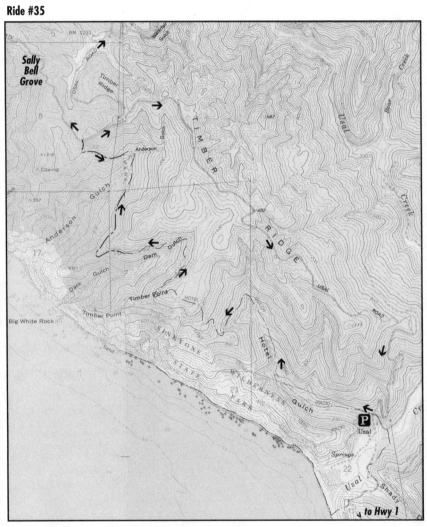

35

Sinkyone Wilderness State Park, Usal Area

Hotel Gulch Bike and Equestrian Trail, with options on Wheeler & Usal Roads

Most of the Sinkyone Wilderness State Park's 7367 acres are off limits to cyclists, but the Usal area, site of an old lumber town, offers variety for self-propelled two wheelers. Usal, one of the most beautiful and remote corners of the Mendocino coast, is a land of breathtaking vistas and towering ridges and cliffs. This moderate ride provides rewards for any cyclist.

Families with young children can enjoy the level roads around the pretty campground and out to the beach. Find a more challenging but still easy ride by driving north on Usal Road 4.5 miles from the campground to the un-marked Wheeler Road, on the left behind an orange gate. From there you can ride downhill 1.1 miles to the remnant virgin redwoods of Sally Bell Grove (see Option 2). Return from there for a 2.1-mile round trip with 240 feet of up and down, or continue another 2 miles, for a 6-mile round trip with about double the elevation change.

Advanced riders without agoraphobia might consider cycling the six miles of steep and twisting dirt road from Highway One to Usal Campground, ideal if you have someone along who'd rather drive than ride. But watch out for traffic, especially on the corkscrew descent to Usal.

The Hotel Gulch Trail follows the eastern park boundary, climbing over Timber Ridge, then dipping through the upper reaches of Dark Gulch and Anderson Gulch before ending at the Wheeler Road. From there you have several choices to extend the loop, as described below.

DIRECTIONS TO STARTING POINT: Turn west off Highway One at M.90.88 (13 miles north of Westport, 16 miles south of Leggett) onto unpaved, sometimes unmarked Usal Road (the first 50 feet from the highway is paved, but not the rest). Go 6 steep, winding miles to Usal Campground, then take the second left after the bridge. This is Hotel Gulch Road, so find a place to park.

123

WARNING!: Watch for and yield to equestrians. Watch for motor vehicles on Usal Road.

ELEVATION AT START: 40 feet

OPTION 1: Hotel Gulch Trail to end (at Wheeler Road) and return. Moderate, 11.6 miles round trip, no vehicle traffic. Elevation Gain/Loss: 2200 feet+/2200 feet-

OPTION 2: Add Wheeler Road to Sally Bell Grove or locked gate and return. Moderate, add 1 or 3 miles round trip, no vehicle traffic. Elevation Gain/Loss: Add 40 feet+/40 feet- to grove; add 500 feet+/ 500 feet- to gate.

OPTION 3: Hotel Gulch Road, Wheeler Road and Usal Road south. Moderate, 11-mile loop, light vehicle traffic on Usal Road. Elevation Gain/Loss: 2660 feet+/2660 feet-

OPTION 4: Add Usal Road north and return. Strenuous, add up to 30 miles or more, light vehicle traffic. Elevation Gain/Loss: Add 430 feet+/430 feet- for 1 mile; add 680 feet+/680 feet- for 2 miles, etc.

SURFACE: Dirt double track

FEE: No day use fee. Camping at Usal: $7–9/camp.

FACILITIES: Pit toilets, tables, fire rings, trash cans at Usal Campground. BRING YOUR OWN WATER.

Ride Notes

Our ride starts at the junction of Usal Road and Hotel Gulch Trail at the north end of Usal Campground. Hotel Gulch Trail, an old logging road, heads west on a gentle incline through forest. Pass a silver gate at .1 mile and climb gradually to .5 mile where you cross a tributary of Hotel Gulch Creek. Ascend moderately on good track to 1.5 miles. At big bends left and right, look south for the first views along the coast.

Encounter water bars after 1.5 miles, continuing a moderate climb with intermittent steep hills. At 1.8 mile the ascent eases at a big bend right where you overlook the nearby Lost Coast Trail and the rugged shoreline beyond. The double track continues its moderate ascent over Timber Ridge, with some gradual inclines providing relief. After another coastal view at 2.1 miles, ascend moderately by switchbacks to top Timber Ridge at 2.6 miles.

At the 1240-foot summit, vistas suddenly expand to include the heavily logged but spectacular watersheds of Dark Gulch and Anderson Gulch to the northwest. As you start to descend, a big bend to the right at 2.7 miles offers views west down steep Dark Gulch to its mouth, where Big White Rock towers offshore. Hotel Gulch Trail descends moderately to 3.3 miles where you cross Dark Gulch. Above the creek crossing, Dark Gulch Creek tumbles over a 12-foot-tall rock shelf draped with five-finger ferns, a lovely weeping wall.

Your double track descends gradually for about a mile. Pause at 4 miles for another great view down Dark Gulch. Look south to Timber Ridge, where several large trees 200 to 300 feet tall pierce the skyline. Imagine this entire watershed filled with an immense forest of redwoods and firs, many with bases twenty feet or more in diameter. Such a forest was here until 1980, and may grow back in another 500 years.

Hotel Gulch Trail bends to the right and crosses to the north side of a ridge, entering the Anderson Gulch watershed. The descent continues until 4.7 miles, where you cross the first of several forks of Anderson Gulch Creek. Ascend moderately through an area where recent restoration and repair of logging damage makes for rough tread. After crossing the creek's main fork at 4.9 miles, climb steeply, with occasional relief, to 5.3 miles. Tread improves as the incline turns moderate to the end of Hotel Gulch Trail at the old Wheeler Road at 5.8 miles, where you have several choices. Options 2 and 4 extend either Option 1 or 3 with tangential rides. Option 3 is a loop. Option 1 retraces your route back over Timber Ridge and down Hotel Gulch.

OPTION 2 goes left at the end of Hotel Gulch Trail to descend the Wheeler Road .5 mile to Sally Bell Grove, a remnant stand of virgin redwoods with a commanding view down Little Jackass Creek to the shore when it is clear. You can continue down Wheeler Road for one mile beyond the grove, where a locked gate marks the end of bicycle access. This stretch offers more coastal views north and south.

OPTION 3 turns right, climbing Wheeler Road to Usal Road, then turns right to loop back to Usal, a short up followed by a long downhill.

OPTION 4 climbs Wheeler Road to Usal Road, then goes left, heading north on Usal Road, a ride that can go on virtually as long as you want, offering steep terrain suitable for cyclists in top shape. The two miles north of Wheeler Road are moderate. Beyond that, Usal Road offers repeated ascents and descents. In 15 rugged miles it reaches Four Corners, where a left turn descends 1300 feet to the northern portion of Sinkyone Wilderness State Park. The Usal Road beyond 2 miles north of Wheeler Road is recommended only for fit, avid cyclists.

125

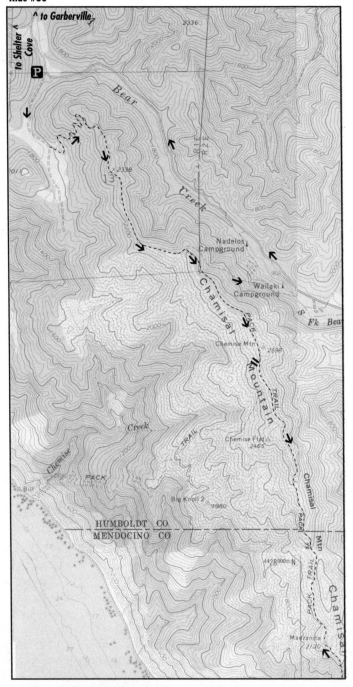

36

Hidden Valley to Chemise Mountain & Beyond

Chemise Mountain Trail

This ride starts in Humboldt County, a long way from the Mendocino coast. But good single track is a rare commodity and this trail has it in spades, some of California's finest. On a clear day Chemise Mountain offers one of the great vistas of the Mendocino coast (Option 3 is mostly in Mendocino County). The route requires advanced riding skills, especially from .5 to 1 mile and beyond 3.3 miles, but if you have moderately good mountain bike skills, you can walk your bike through the tight switchbacks in the first mile and enjoy the mostly moderate track of Options 1 and 2. Don't ride beyond 3.3 miles unless you accept full responsibility for your neck.

If you can stay longer in Humboldt, get the BLM (707/ 825-2300) map of King Range National Conservation Area, the 60,000-acre jewel with Chemise Mountain in its southwest corner. Check out Paradise Ridge Road, King Range Road, Saddle Mountain Road or Smith-Etter Road for some rugged double track through great country. If you still want more, my Hiker's hip pocket Guide to the Humboldt Coast *describes a dozen other trails open to bikes.*

DIRECTIONS TO STARTING POINT: Leave Highway 101 at Garberville (M.10.8). Take Redwood Drive 2.8 miles to Redway, then take Briceland Road west 17.5 miles. Take Chemise Mountain Road .25 mile to Hidden Valley Trailhead on right.

ELEVATION AT START: 1700 feet

OPTION 1: Hidden Valley to Chemise Mountain.
Advanced, 5.2 miles round trip.
Elevation Gain/Loss: 1150 feet+/1150 feet-

OPTION 2: Hidden Valley, Chemise Mountain, Wailaki Loop.
Advanced, 7.2-mile semi-loop, light vehicle traffic on last leg.
Elevation Gain/Loss: 1030 feet+/1030 feet-

127

OPTION 3: Hidden Valley to Manzanita Peak.

Very advanced, 8 or 12 miles round trip.

Elevation Gain/Loss: 2180 feet+/ 2180 feet- to Manzanita, 3300 feet+/ 3300 feet- to park boundary.

SURFACE: Dirt single track

FACILITIES: Campground with pit toilets and water 1.4 miles south on Chemise Mountain Road (camping: $8/night; day use: $1).

Ride Notes

Ride around the green gate and follow a level double track overgrown with mint and riparian vegetation. Cross a tiny creek and come to the lush meadow of Hidden Valley, with Pacific views south and west. Where the track forks at .25 mile, go left and ascend bumpy single track. (The right fork meanders through Hidden Valley, ending before .5 mile.) Ford a seasonal creek at .4 mile and come to a signed switchback overlooking Hidden Valley's apple orchard.

The advanced riding starts as narrow single track switches left over a sandstone shelf and ascends steeply. The most difficult and technical parts of Option 1 occur in the half-mile ascent to the ridge. Recross the creek and ascend three switchbacks to a small rest bench at .6 mile. The ride gets tougher as you climb by five more short, tight switchbacks to .7 mile. Contour briefly through burned forest, then ascend fitfully. After a sharp switchback to the left, ascend steeply but fitfully by three more switchbacks, gaining a saddle on the ridgetop before 1 mile.

Switchback right and ascend steeply on the ridgetop. Snowy peaks appear to the east as you pass two large, fire-scarred firs. Contour and ascend fitfully to 1.2 miles. Dip, rise and dip again along the ridgetop to 1.4 miles, then repeat the pattern to 1.6 miles. Big roots break up the tread at the base of a short steep rise. Then contour and rise through a brush field with sweeping ocean views. Ascend to a junction at 1.9 miles.

The fork on the left descends to Wailaki and Nadelos Campgrounds (Option 2). Turn right and continue up the ridge through forest. In April 1996 several downed trees required a detour uphill around 2.3 miles. Ascend moderately to the ridgetop at 2.4 miles, then gradually. After a short steep rise, reach the trail's summit at 2.6 miles, 2560 feet above sea level. You might park your bike and walk a vague, overgrown track on the left that winds 150 feet to Chemise Mountain's 2598-foot summit. The top offers a sweeping view east to the 7000-foot summits of the Yolla Bolly Mountains and south over deep Whale Gulch to the rugged shore of Sinkyone Wilderness State Park, the Mendocino coast sprawling seaward beyond.

OPTIONS 1 & 2 return from here. Option 1 retraces your entire route, a 5.2-mile round trip. Option 2 returns to the junction at 3.3 miles, then turns right and descends moderately, then steeply southeast on narrow tread across a steep slope. Stay right at the junction with Nadelos Trail at 5.1 miles, continuing a steady descent east to Wailaki Campground at 5.35 miles. Turn left and ride the level campground road to Chemise Mountain Road, then go left 1.6 miles (watch for traffic) to the starting point.

OPTION 3: The Chemise Mountain Trail continues south along the ridge, offering rocky but good tread with minimal elevation change to 3.3 miles. Contour and descend gradually to 2.7 miles, where you have a view of Shelter Cove to the west. Ascend briefly to a knob, then dip and rise along the ridgetop to another knob shaded by young firs at 3 miles. Ascend fitfully to brushy Chemise Flat at 3.1 miles, then start a gradual descent with views south into the Sinkyone.

By 3.3 miles you want to turn back unless you're a very skilled and fit rider. The descent turns steep and winding on eroded tread with patches of loose rock, a technically challenging and unforgiving combination. If you continue, from 3.4 miles the trail rises, dips and rises to another top at 3.5 miles. By 3.6 miles only technical skills will prevent disaster as the trail drops steeply on uneven and loose rocky tread. Ascend briefly to 3.8 miles, then drop steeply on shaded tread, before rising briefly to the summit called Manzanita at 4 miles. A USGS bench marker on the right states your elevation as 2120 feet. An expansive view looks south over the convoluted terrain of Sinkyone Wilderness.

If you're still game to continue, you can go another 2 miles down the ridge to the state park boundary, where you are required to turn back and ascend steeply back to Chemise Mountain. From Manzanita, rough narrow track descends southeast, dropping steeply by switchbacks through mature fir forest in a gully around 4.3 miles, then contouring back to the ridgetop. Descend steeply along the ridgetop, then rise to a top beyond 4.7 miles. The tread descends fitfully across gentler terrain to 5.4 miles, then drops steeply again, only to ascend steeply along a razor ridgetop. Drop then ascend through grasslands, then descend steeply through forest. At 5.9 miles the trail descends through grasslands, soon merging with a road and rising to a flat clearing at 6 miles. Please turn back here as the park boundary is just beyond.

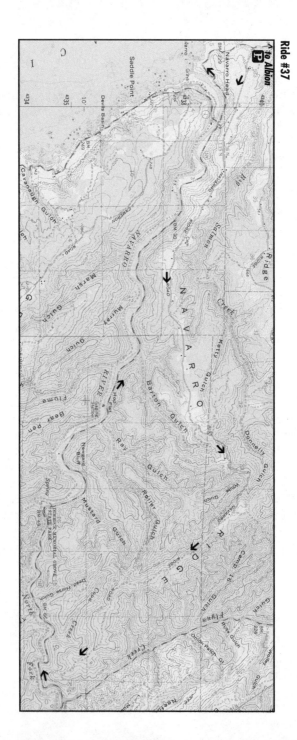

130

37

Navarro Ridge

Navarro Ridge Road, with option on Highways 128 & One

This scenic ridgetop route offers some of the prettiest country and vistas on the Mendocino coast. Navarro Ridge Road was built in the 1850s as the original stagecoach route between Anderson Valley and Mendocino, far more reliable than following the flood-prone Navarro River as Highway 128 does today. Fortunately traffic is light these days, though be wary of vehicles speeding, or not watching for cyclists. Option 1 explores the easiest, loveliest and most heavily traveled section of the ridge. If you continue east, the traffic becomes very light and the terrain turns more challenging. The whole ride is pleasant, except perhaps the rigorous ascent around 8 miles.

DIRECTIONS TO STARTING POINT: Navarro Ridge Road heads east from Highway One south of Albion at M.42.35. Park in the wide turnout on the west side of the highway. You can also park at the east end of Navarro Ridge and ride west. It is on Highway 128 at M.11.6, just west of Flynn Creek Road between Navarro and the coast.

ELEVATION AT START: 230 feet

OPTION 1: Navarro Ridge Road to 5.9 miles and return.
Easy, 11.8 miles round trip, light vehicle traffic.
Elevation Gain/Loss: 750 feet+/750 feet-

OPTION 2: Navarro Ridge Road to 11.5 miles and return.
Moderate, 23 miles round trip, light vehicle traffic.
Elevation Gain/Loss: 2470 feet+/2470 feet-

OPTION 3: Entire length of Navarro Ridge Road and return.
Strenuous, 26.8 miles round trip, light vehicle traffic.
Elevation Gain/Loss: 3650 feet+/3650 feet-

OPTION 4: East on Navarro Ridge Road, return west on Highway 128 and Highway One.

Strenuous, 27-mile loop, light vehicle traffic, except Highways One and 128, heavy traffic.

Elevation Gain/Loss: 2050 feet+/2050 feet-

SURFACE: Mixed, paved and dirt roads

FACILITIES: Option 4 only — Dimmick Campground on Highway 128

Ride Notes

From the broad turnout on the west side of Highway One, Navarro Ridge Road is .1 mile south. For simplicity, our described ride starts from the Highway One intersection. Ascend east on the two-lane pavement of Navarro Ridge Road, climbing moderately, even steeply for .3 mile. After passing historic Fensalden Inn, once a stagecoach stop, the ascent turns gradual as you gain the ridgetop. Look to the right around 1 mile for a spectacular view to the mouth of the Navarro River. From 1.7 miles, contour along the ridgetop with views left and right. Descend slightly around 2.2 miles, then resume a fitful ascent, with the steepest hill around 2.5 miles. Most of your climb is gradual as the road narrows to one lane.

Descend briefly from 3.5 miles on narrow, winding pavement through redwood forest, then cross a wooden bridge where the terrain on your left drops steeply to Salmon Creek. Then it's up and down through pastures until the end of the pavement at 4.1 miles. Contour on gravel tread with intermittent pavement, then continue on dirt and gravel through easy ups and downs. At 5.9 miles, a square school bus turnaround is on the right. It makes a good place to turn back for easy Option 1.

OPTIONS 2, 3 & 4: Continue east past Navarro Ridge Ranch, where a sign warning "Through traffic not advised" refers to vehicle traffic, though downed trees farther up the ridgetop may thwart cyclists in winter. The narrow double track rises and dips twice to 6.8 miles, where you have views north over the gulches at the head of Big Salmon Creek. Ascend gradually to a stump ranch at 7 miles, then climb moderately. Drop moderately to the head of White Gulch at 7.7 miles, then begin a sustained moderate ascent with some steep pitches, finally leveling at 1120 feet on the ridgetop at 8.4 miles.

Navarro Ridge Road hugs the ridgetop for the next 2.5 miles, staying between 1000 and 1150 feet in elevation. After a short downhill, rise to a second summit at 8.7 miles, then descend past the eastern-most residence on Navarro Ridge. A sign at 8.9 miles indicates "Road not maintained in winter," and it's the next section that may be blocked by downed trees after storms. You'll need to navigate some water bars year round and mudholes in spring, but if fallen trees don't block your route, you can follow the ridgetop road on an easy segment with little elevation change and expansive views. Between 10 and 11.5 miles the road rises above 1100 feet four times, with a dip between each top. The final top, where a private road forks right to descend Roller Gulch, is a good place to turn back unless you are making the loop on Highway 128.

OPTIONS 3 & 4: For a strenuous round trip or loop, continue south-east and east on Navarro Ridge Road. After a brief ascent, descend steadily with the ridgetop. Rise to one more knob of nearly 1000 feet around 12 miles, then continue a mostly gradual descent. By 13 miles, make a steep winding descent off the end of the ridge, dropping into the canyon of Flynn Creek. Navarro Ridge Road ends at Highway 128, right beside Flynn Creek, 13.4 miles from your starting point. Option 3 returns the way you came, easily the more arduous but less trafficked of the two choices.

OPTION 4: If you don't mind contending with high-speed traffic, Highway 128's 11.6 miles to the coast and Highway One's steep ascent to Navarro Head and your starting point offer great scenery. You've probably driven Highway 128 through Navarro River Redwoods State Park, but it's a different experience altogether to cycle it. The nearly level route winds through dense redwood forest along the canyon of North Fork Navarro River until Dimmick Campground at 17 miles. There you meet the main stem of the Navarro, following it past numer-ous inviting swimming holes to the coast. You can't see the pools from the road, but they might be marked by a mass of parked cars on a hot day. Some of the best are between 18.3 and 19.7 miles.

Highway 128 ends 25 miles into your ride. Follow Highway One up the twisting Navarro River grade, with spectacular views of the coast and the river's mouth. The last mile contours over Navarro Head. Return to your starting point at 27 miles.

38

Navarro River at Hendy Woods

Park road & Navarro River fire road, with options on Ray's Road, Highway 128, Highland Ranch road & Greenwood Road

This easy ride traverses the length of Hendy Woods State Park, offering big redwoods, tiny creeks and the Navarro River for great scenery. Two longer options loop through the tiny hamlet of Philo and return via Highway 128 (Option 3), or loop back over hills above the park through secluded Highland Ranch (Option 4). The latter two options are possible through a generous mutual-use agreement with three lodgings along the route. Please stay on the route and respect the privacy of people at Wellspring Renewal Center, Shenoa Retreat and Highland Ranch.

Note: For a treat, consider a stay at one of these rural retreats. Wellspring (707/ 895-3893) and Shenoa (707/ 895-3156) are rustic, while Highland Ranch (707/ 895-3600) is deluxe.

DIRECTIONS TO STARTING POINT: From Highway 128 west of Philo at M.20.15, turn onto Philo-Greenwood Road. Go .5 mile and park beyond the Navarro River bridge. (Hendy Woods State Park entrance is uphill on the left. You can also pay to enter park, drive to end of park road and start from there as described in Option 2, or start from park campground if you camp there.)

WARNING!: Bikes not allowed on the park's single track trails.

ELEVATION AT START: 200 feet

OPTION 1: From Navarro River parking near park entrance, park road, Navarro River Fire Road to slide near southern park boundary.
Easy, 6 miles round trip, light vehicle traffic.
Elevation Gain/Loss: 440 feet+/440 feet-

OPTION 2: Navarro River Fire Road from Hendy Picnic Area to slide near southern park boundary.
Easy, 3.2 miles round trip, minimal vehicle traffic.
Elevation Gain/Loss: 160 feet+/160 feet-

OPTION 3: Loop through Philo.
Easy, 8.3-mile loop, light vehicle traffic except highway — heavy traffic.
Elevation Gain/Loss: 560 feet+/560 feet-

OPTION 4: Loop through Highland Ranch.
Moderate, 10.3-mile loop, light vehicle traffic.
Elevation Gain/Loss: 1260 feet+/1260 feet-

SURFACE: Mixed, dirt and paved roads

FEE: $5/vehicle, day use parking to drive into Hendy Woods.

FACILITIES: Picnic area, campground, restrooms, water, phone in park; store, cafe, fruit stands, wineries on Highway 128.

Ride #38

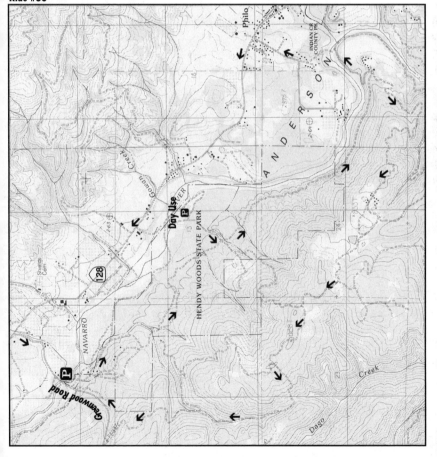

Ride Notes

Ride uphill away from the river on Greenwood Road. Before .1 mile, turn left into Hendy Woods State Park and follow the park road on a gentle ascent, then contour to the entrance kiosk at .4 mile, where you can ask for a map of the "9-mile loop." The meandering, paved park road ascends, topping a hill at .75 mile. Descend, then climb over another small hill before 1.2 miles, then dip and rise again to 1.5 miles.

As you descend moderately from this hilltop, watch on your right for the easy-to-miss fire road at 1.6 miles. Leave the pavement there and take the gravel track behind the silver gate, marked "Bikes OK." (**OPTION 2** starts from the picnic area at the end of the park road, following the park road uphill .2 mile to the fire road.) The fire road contours on good gravel track with occasional gentle ascents. You might glimpse the virgin redwoods of Big Hendy Grove downhill on your left.

Pass another fire road on your right at 1.9 miles, but continue on the gravel track contouring through forest. Ascend a short hill at 2.1 miles and cross a creek. You soon climb more frequently, passing redwoods to seven feet in diameter. At 2.5 miles a fallen redwood hangs overhead. You can see the Navarro River below on your left.

Pass a signed horse trail on the left at 2.7 miles. If the day is hot, you might lock your bike to a small tree and walk the trail to the river to get wet. After the fire road crosses a tiny creek with woodwardia ferns, pedal up the first significant hill. Pass the remnants of a gate at 3 miles and come to a massive slide that has obliterated the road bed. The easiest option retraces your route to the starting point.

OPTIONS 3 & 4: If you are sure-footed enough to continue, you can lift your bike over the rugged slide, following a narrow path underneath two fallen redwoods. It's not easy lifting your bike over the gully just before the end of the slide. Be careful! Beyond the slide the fire road continues a gradual climb on natural tread. By 3.2 miles you come to a silver gate at the southern park boundary. The fire road continues on private property. Please stay on the route and do not disturb occupants if you continue.

The dirt road contours along the river terrace over the lands of Wellspring Renewal Center. Descend fitfully on uneven tread, then climb on rocky tread. The track drops and rises again, then descends to a junction with a road open to motor vehicles at 3.8 miles. Shenoa Retreat is straight ahead. Option 3 goes left at the junction, Option 4 goes right.

OPTION 3: Go left on the road, descending through a big bend to the right, then contouring along the edge of the river terrace. Before 4.2 miles you make a short descent to the river. From May through November, go left across the seasonal bridge over the river. (In winter, fork right and walk your bike across the pedestrian bridge. Follow the road (short single track for winter route) north past Van Zandt's Resort, veer right and soon come to pavement. This is Ray's Road, which contours into Philo and ends at Highway 128 at 5 miles.

Our described loop goes left on busy Highway 128. But you might want to turn right for the short detour into Philo where a store and cafe have provisions. Highway 128 climbs west over a small hill, then descends gradually, paralleling the Navarro River around 6.4 miles. Consider a stop at Gowan's fruit stand around 7 miles, before pedaling up another short hill. At 7.8 miles turn left on Greenwood Road and descend to 8.3 miles to complete the loop.

OPTION 4: If you turn right at the junction at 3.8 miles, be prepared for a 1.3-mile sustained ascent, followed by ups and downs with a total ascent of 900 feet in the next 5.5 miles. OK?

Ascend moderately past improbably placed tennis courts, then through redwood forest. At 4.4 miles bend right and climb away from the redwoods, following the slopes of Dago Creek through mixed forest. Your moderate ascent turns steep around 4.7 miles, again around 5.1 miles.

By 5.2 miles you descend slightly, coming to Highland Ranch. Drop past the main ranch house of this plush but relaxed resort at 5.4 miles, then ascend a short moderate hill. At 5.6 miles bear to the right of a pond on a slight descent, then start a fitful ascent circumnavigating the pond through grasslands. Climb moderately from 6 to 6.3 miles. Then your ascent turns gradual, broken by two short drops. Pass Dutchman's Pond at 6.4 miles, then top out and descend to a fork at 6.6 miles.

Stay right at the fork for a brief ascent, then descend moderately almost to 7 miles. Ascend fitfully on uneven tread through mixed forest, contour around 7.4 miles, then begin a long descent. It drops fitfully, mostly moderate with a few steep sections. By 8.1 miles the long downhill turns gradual on a winding road.

Descent turns to contour by 8.6 miles. When you ascend gradually to cross a creek at 9 miles, power up and be ready to gear down on one last moderate ascent to 9.3 miles. That leads to a contour with easy ups and downs until you drop to paved Greenwood Road at 9.8 miles. Turn right and watch for traffic as you descend to the Hendy Woods Park entrance at 10.3 miles to complete the loop.

39

Anderson Valley

Anderson Valley Way, with option on Highway 128

This easy meander along a quiet country lane allows a relaxed look at Anderson Valley's pastoral landscape tucked amidst the rolling hills of the Coast Range. Gentle terrain and minimal traffic as you roll past pastures, vineyards and orchards make the ride a suitable excursion for families.

DIRECTIONS TO STARTING POINT: Off Highway 128 between Boonville and Philo, Anderson Valley Way (old Highway 128) can be reached at M.25.3 east of Philo or at M.28 just west of Boonville. Park on the road shoulder at either broad intersection.

ELEVATION AT START: 290 feet

OPTION 1: Anderson Valley Way from one highway access to another.
Easy, 5.4 miles round trip, light vehicle traffic.
Elevation Gain/Loss: 120 feet+/120 feet-

OPTION 2: Add ride into Boonville.
Easy, add 2.2 miles round trip, medium highway and town traffic.
Elevation Gain/Loss: Add 120 feet+/120 feet-

OPTION 3: Entire length of Anderson Valley Way.
Easy, 6.7 miles round trip, light vehicle traffic.
Elevation Gain/Loss: 200 feet+/200 feet-

SURFACE: Paved county road

FACILITIES: Anderson Valley Historical Museum in a one-room schoolhouse, open Friday–Sunday afternoons, offers exhibits on valley lore. The Tinman on the west end offers organic juices and picnic supplies. Restaurants and cafes in Boonville.

Ride Notes

While you can start from either end, I prefer to start on the Philo end as described here. Contour southeast on Anderson Valley Way from the Highway 128 access road. By .2 mile you pass the Tinman, where organic juices and picnic supplies are available in season. Continue on the winding way through gentle dips and rises past horse pastures. From .7 to .9 mile, pedal up the only significant hill on this span of former highway.

Ride alongside the highway briefly, then drop slightly past Anderson Creek Inn, a B&B for adults. After crossing tiny Con Creek, look for the museum in the little red schoolhouse on your left. (If the flag is flying, it's open.) By 1.7 miles you contour, with views over the gravel beds of Anderson Creek on your right. Dip down to cross Graveyard Creek, passing Evergreen Cemetery, then a hodgepodge of old and new houses.

Ride #39

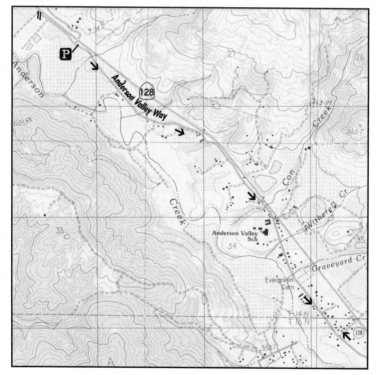

At 2.7 miles Anderson Valley Way forks. The left fork returns to Highway 128, while the right fork quickly ends. Option 1 returns from here, following Anderson Valley Way back to your starting point.

OPTION 2: To extend your ride into the little town of Boonville, take the left fork. Turn right and cautiously ride the shoulder of Highway 128. It's about one mile to the center of town. Picnic supplies are available at Boont Berry Farm and Anderson Valley Market, or you can choose from several eateries ranging from simple to fancy. Return the way you came.

OPTION 3: If you get back to your starting point and want a short cool-down ride, Anderson Valley Way contours northwest for .5 mile to its end, a 1-mile round trip. A more challenging option would be to follow Highway 128 into tiny Philo, almost 3 miles each way, where you could link with Ride #38, Option 3, or stop for picnic supplies or wine tasting before returning to your starting point.

40

Headwaters of South Fork Big River

Comptche-Ukiah Road to Montgomery Woods, Orr Springs & beyond

This is the Jekyll and Hyde of paved rides. If you like easy terrain, start at the South Fork Big River bridge 24.5 miles from Highway One. You'll ride up the lovely gentle bottom of the steep-sloped canyon of that coastal river, many meandering miles from where Big River empties into the Pacific Ocean at Mendocino Bay. Best of all, the Jekyll ride culminates at the inspiring virgin redwood groves of Montgomery Woods State Reserve, where you can lock your bike and walk an easy 1½-mile loop trail to the biggest trees, or continue another easy and scenic 2 miles along the pavement to Orr Hot Springs Resort (reservations required to visit).

The ride's hairy Mr. Hyde side emerges if you continue beyond Orr Springs, where a steep ascent gains 800 feet in the first mile, a total of 1500 feet in around 4 miles. If you like challenging ascents, you'll love this one through oak spattered grasslands, with some stunning views from the top end. A thrilling descent beckons in either direction! It's an 1800-foot drop in the 6 miles back to Montgomery Woods, about 1900 feet down to Ukiah if you continue east — consider a shuttle. Another Hyde-bound choice is to start from the Comptche Store, adding a steep ascent and descent in each direction, as described in Option 3.

DIRECTIONS TO STARTING POINT: Turn east off Highway One at M.50.00 onto Comptche-Ukiah Road. Go 24.5 winding miles (1 mile on dirt) to the bridge over South Fork Big River. Park on road shoulder.

ELEVATION AT START: 480 feet

OPTION 1: Lower bridge, South Fork Big River to Montgomery Woods. Easy, 10.2 miles round trip, light to medium vehicle traffic. Elevation Gain/Loss: 550 feet+/550 feet-

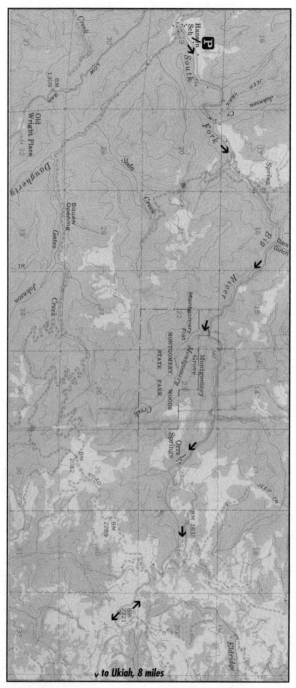

v to Ukiah, 8 miles

OPTION 2: Continue east from Montgomery Woods.

Easy, add 4 miles round trip to Orr Hot Springs, or strenuous, up to 30 miles round trip to end of road at Ukiah, light to medium vehicle traffic.

Elevation Gain/Loss: 730 feet+/730 feet- round trip to Orr, 2190 feet+/2130 feet- one way to Ukiah.

OPTION 3: Start from Comptche Store (elevation 183 feet)

Strenuous, add 20 miles round trip, light to medium vehicle traffic.

Elevation Gain/Loss: 2320 feet+/2320 feet-

SURFACE: Paved, except 1 mile of dirt on Option 3.

FACILITIES: Picnic areas and pit toilets at Montgomery Woods State Reserve; hot springs, cabins and camping at Orr Springs Resort (must call for reservations before you go, 707/ 462-6277).

Ride Notes

This scenic country lane makes a gentle ascent through pasture lands surrounded by dark forests. After a brief contour around 1 mile, several short slight descents break up the gradual uphill. You get frequent glimpses of the river on your right winding through the woods.

Watch out for the cattle guard at 2.3 miles, then pass an odd square sawdust burner from an old sawmill. After a gradual ascent, contour to 3 miles, then climb again. Pastures become scarce as the canyon deepens. None of the ascents are steep, but each uphill is followed by a short descent. The last brief downhill at 5 miles leads to a sturdy bridge crossing the river. Suddenly you arrive at the parking lot for Montgomery Woods. If you park your bike, you can walk the trail to toilets, tables and the biggest trees. To complete Option 1, return the way you came.

OPTION 2: If you continue east, use caution on a particularly narrow stretch of road. Ascend gently along the beautiful South Fork beneath big redwoods and Douglas firs. After another bridge at 5.3 miles, contour through a clearing with pioneer apple trees, then past fern draped boulders above the river's mossy banks. Cross a creek flowing from the north at 6 miles, pass big redwoods and cross another bridge where the river flows over polished stone. The river's larger fork swings north as you follow a smaller tributary. Ascend gradually around 6.5 miles, soon pedaling over bumpy pavement. If you pass Orr Springs, established 1858, at 7.1 miles, the ascent rapidly turns from moderate to steep.

Struggle through several switchbacks as you climb into oak woodlands. If you continue, watch out for several more cattle guards on the steep ascent. As you reach 2000 feet around 9 miles, the worst of the climb is over. You leave the Big River watershed for that of the Russian River. The ride's 2540-foot summit is about 11 miles from the starting point. If you continue east from there, it is virtually all downhill to road's end in Ukiah at 20 miles.

OPTION 3: If you like long rides and fairly punishing terrain, consider starting at the Comptche Store, 15 miles west of Montgomery Woods. The first 2 miles are easy uphill through a pastoral landscape. The vegetation turns to chaparral as you ascend steeply to the 1240-foot summit at 3.8 miles. Then it's roller coaster time — descend moderately to 4.3 miles, climb back to 1200 feet at 5.2 miles, followed by four shorter down-up runs, the last one topping out once again at 1240 feet at 7.2 miles. Contour on the ridgetop for .5 mile with grand views south, drop steeply around 8 miles, then pass Low Gap Road at 8.5 miles. (Low Gap Road, mostly unpaved, follows ridges before descending a canyon to reach Ukiah in 21 miles.) Start a descent that turns steep as the pavement ends at 8.8 miles for a bumpy downhill on broad track. At 9.9 miles the pavement resumes as you cross the bridge over South Fork Big River and come to the starting point for Option 1.

41

Gualala Ridge

Old State Highway, Old Stage Road, with options on Pacific Woods Road, Fish Rock Road, Iversen Road, Ten Mile Cutoff Road, Ten Mile Road, Eureka Hill Road & Highway One

This ride climbs steeply in its first mile to gain a ridgetop and follow the original Gualala to Point Arena stagecoach route. It's a pleasant and popular ride through a rural residential area, offering grand views over the ocean and coastal watersheds. You can follow the ridge up to a dozen miles without dropping below 800 feet. If the first mile sounds too steep, drive to Bower Park and start there. (A 5-mile ride north to Iversen Road/Ten Mile Cutoff Road junction and back — 10.1 miles round trip — has only 810 feet of elevation change.) More challenging options drop down side roads to loop back to Gualala along Highway One.

DIRECTIONS TO STARTING POINT: On Highway One at the south end of Gualala, the ride starts at the highway's intersection with Old State Highway. (Parking is limited at the intersection. You can park .5 mile south at a wide turnout on the east side of Highway One north of the Gualala River bridge.)

ELEVATION AT START: 40 feet

OPTION 1: Old State Highway, Old Stage Road to Bower Park and return.
Easy, 6.4 miles round trip, medium vehicle traffic.
Elevation Gain/Loss: 900 feet+/900 feet-

OPTION 2: Loop back on Pacific Woods Road and Highway One.
Easy, 4.8-mile loop, medium vehicle traffic, except Highway One — heavy traffic.
Elevation Gain/Loss: 800 feet+/800 feet-

OPTION 3: Loop back on Fish Rock Road and Highway One.
Moderate, 13.7-mile loop, medium vehicle traffic, except Highway One — heavy traffic.
Elevation Gain/Loss: 1665 feet+/1665 feet-

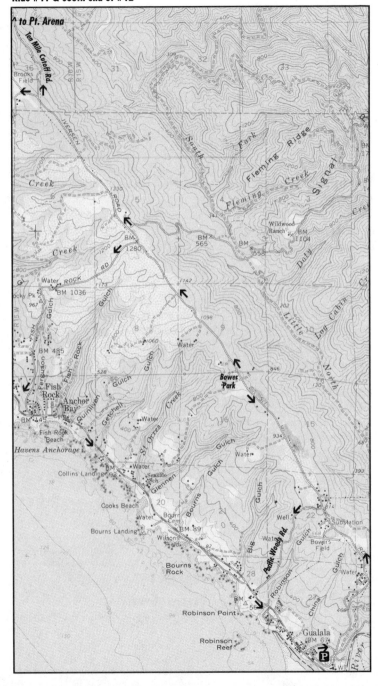

OPTION 4: Loop back on Iversen Road and Highway One.

Moderate, 22.1-mile loop, medium vehicle traffic, except Highway One — heavy traffic.

Elevation Gain/Loss: 2210 feet+/2210 feet-

OPTION 5: Old State Highway, Old Stage Road, Ten Mile Cutoff Road, Ten Mile Road, Eureka Hill Road to Point Arena.

Strenuous, 17 miles one way, 34.1 miles round trip or return via Highway One for a 32-mile loop, medium vehicle traffic.

Elevation Gain/Loss: 2000 feet+/1840 feet- one way, 3840 feet+/3840 feet- round trip, 3100 feet+/3100 feet- for loop.

SURFACE: Paved county roads

FACILITIES: Bower Park has restrooms, water, phone and picnic tables, plus tennis courts and a nice playground. Grocery stores and delicatessens in Gualala, Anchor Bay and Point Arena stock provisions.

Ride Notes

Head east from Highway One on two-lane Old State Highway, climbing gently. At .3 mile, veer left on Old Stage Road and climb steeply on the winding two-lane road with no shoulder. Beyond one mile you gain the ridge and the ascent turns moderate. At 2.3 miles, where you've reached an elevation of 820 feet, Pacific Woods Road is on the left. (**OPTION 2:** Pacific Woods offers a short loop, descending moderately, then steeply to Highway One at the north end of Gualala.)

Continuing up Old Stage Road, the ascent turns gradual on the way to Bower Community Park, on your left at 3.2 miles. The small park offers a pleasant rest stop amidst redwood and hardwood forest with some sunny clearings. If you've had enough climbing and prefer not riding on Highway One, Option 1 retraces your route back to Gualala, a 6.4-mile round trip.

OPTIONS 3, 4 & 5: Old Stage Road continues north along the ridge, making a series of gradual ascents interspersed with short descents. Beyond 4.5 miles, ascend steadily until the junction with Fish Rock Road on your left at 6.2 miles.

OPTION 3: Fish Rock Road offers a steep and winding, paved 2.9-mile descent to Highway One just north of the little town of Anchor Bay (groceries and cafe), from which it is 4.6 miles south along busy Highway One to your starting point.

OPTIONS 4 & 5: If you're game for a longer ride, continue north along the ridgetop route. In only .2 mile you'll pass Fish Rock Road where it heads east. (While that route does meander east for 27 miles to end at Highway 128 near Yorkville, it is not recommended for anyone but advanced gonzo riders — the first mile, paved, drops 700 feet, then the road turns to rough gravel/dirt as it climbs tortuously to 2200 feet elevation before its 6-mile point.)

Back on the ridgetop beyond Fish Rock Road, the two-lane blacktop changes its name to Iversen Road and climbs gradually to its high point of 1330 feet at 7.5 miles. The route dips, resumes climbing to 8.2 miles, then dips again, coming to an important junction at 8.25 miles.

OPTION 4: The left fork is Iversen Road. It climbs for .25 mile to 1370 feet, then starts a gradual, winding descent. After one short up at 8.8 miles, descend steeply, with sweeping Pacific Ocean views on clear days. The descent eases along a straightaway around 10 miles. Take it easy beyond 10.6 as the drop increases, turning steep around 11 miles. You reach busy Highway One at 12.75 miles. Just .5 mile north along the highway is Iversen Point, where a side road drops to a pretty spot on open headlands overlooking the Pacific. But save energy and time for the 9.3-mile run down heavily traveled Highway One to your starting point, completing a 22-mile loop.

OPTION 5: The fork on the right at 8.25 miles, called Ten Mile Cutoff Road, descends steeply to 9.2 miles, then roller coasters to 13.2 miles before dropping steeply again to reach Point Arena and Highway One 17 miles from Gualala. For details, see Ride #42.

42

Ridges Inland from Point Arena

Eureka Hill Road, Ten Mile Road, Ten Mile Cutoff Road with options on Schooner Gulch Road, Iversen Road, Fish Rock Road, Old Stage Road & Highway One

The ridge above Point Arena, once the stage route to Gualala, provides cyclists with a pleasant, usually sunny route. Start from town, making the moderate ascent as described below, or park somewhere along the ridge for an easier ride. Most of the options descend side roads to loop back on Highway One, or you can ride all the way to Gualala. Option 5 offers a strenuous ascent on pavement, following Eureka Hill Road to its end atop Eureka Hill and returning by a steep and wild twisting descent.

DIRECTIONS TO STARTING POINT: On Highway One just north of downtown Point Arena, park where Eureka Hill Road/Riverside Drive heads east.

ELEVATION AT START: 180 feet

OPTION 1: Eureka Hill Road, Ten Mile Road to head of Schooner Gulch and return.
Moderate, 11.8 miles round trip, medium vehicle traffic.
Elevation Gain/Loss: 1450 feet+/1450 feet-

OPTION 2: Eureka Hill Road, Ten Mile Road, Schooner Gulch Road and Highway One.
Moderate, 12.7-mile loop, medium vehicle traffic, except Highway One — heavy traffic.
Elevation Gain/Loss: 1665 feet+/1665 feet-

OPTION 3: Eureka Hill Road, Ten Mile Road, Ten Mile Cutoff Road, Iversen Road and Highway One.
Moderate, 19-mile loop, medium vehicle traffic, except Highway One — heavy traffic.
Elevation Gain/Loss: 2135 feet+/2135 feet-

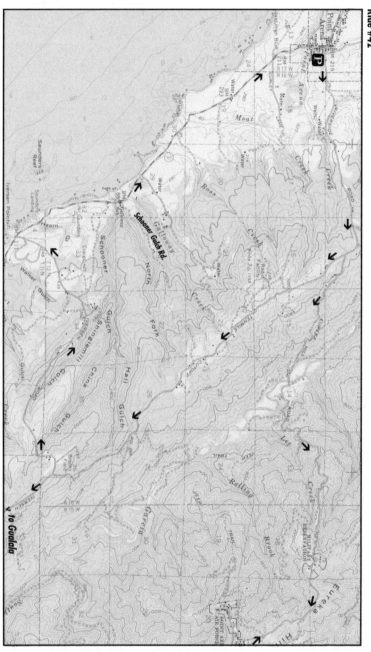

OPTION 4: Riverside Drive, Eureka Hill Road, Ten Mile Road, Ten Mile Cutoff Road, Old Stage Road to Gualala and return.

Strenuous, 17 miles one way, 34.1 miles round trip or return via Highway One for a 32-mile loop, medium vehicle traffic.

Elevation Gain/Loss: 1840 feet+/2000 feet- one way, 3840 feet+/ 3840 feet- round trip, 3100 feet+/3100 feet- for loop.

OPTION 5: Riverside Drive, Eureka Hill Road to river or end and return, light to medium vehicle traffic.

Moderate, 9.5 miles round trip to Garcia River or strenuous, 21.2 miles round trip, light to medium vehicle traffic.

Elevation Gain/Loss: 1450 feet+/1450 feet- to river, 3850 feet+/3850 feet- to end.

SURFACE: Paved (Schooner Gulch Road, Option 2, is gravel).

FACILITIES: At Schooner Gulch unit of Mendocino coast state parks, M.11.4 on Highway One, a pit toilet is .1 mile down the trail from the highway. Stores in Point Arena have provisions.

Ride Notes

This ride starts where Riverside Drive leaves Highway One just north of downtown Point Arena. As you ascend gradually east, Riverside becomes Eureka Hill Road. Two short descents interrupt your climb in the first 1.1 miles. Climb sharply, then moderately to 2 miles followed by a steep ascent to 2.75 miles.

At 3.1 miles, Eureka Hill Road veers left for a steep descent, described below in Option 5. All other options turn right on Ten Mile Road for a moderate ascent to 3.8 miles. Over the next 2 miles, Ten Mile Road dips and rises three times, with no net gain in elevation. At 5.9 miles Schooner Gulch Road is on your right. Option 1 takes the easiest route, turning back to retrace your route to Point Arena.

OPTION 2 descends moderately and steeply along graveled and sometimes bumpy Schooner Gulch Road to 8.7 miles where it ends at Highway One (M.11.4). Across the highway, the Schooner Gulch/Bowling Ball Beach unit of Mendocino coast state parks offers beach, tidepools, headlands and toilet. Turn right for a 4-mile run north along busy Highway One, with one extended moderate climb, to return to Point Arena.

OPTIONS 3 & 4 continue on Ten Mile Road along the ridge up and down on a gentle roller-coaster run. Before 7 miles you dip about 200 feet, then resume roller coastering. From 8 miles, your road (now called

Ten Mile Cutoff Road) ascends steeply to 8.8 miles, where you meet Iversen Road.

OPTION 3 turns right on Iversen, climbing briefly before descending steadily on a pleasant, winding run to road's end at Highway One. A right turn follows busy Highway One north, winding along the coast for about 5.5 miles to return to your starting point at 19 miles.

OPTION 4 turns left at the ridgetop intersection onto Iversen Road, following it along the ridge crest. Pass the route's high point (1330 feet) around 9.5 miles, then descend gradually. At 10.8 miles, Fish Rock Road is on your right. (You can descend steeply on Fish Rock Road, looping back on Highway One, a 24-mile circuit.) Option 4 descends gradually along the ridge road, now called Old Stage Road. At 13.8 miles, Bower Community Park on your right offers picnic tables, drinking water, phone and shady forest. You can continue on a moderate and steep descent to 17 miles and road's end at Highway One on the south end of Gualala, where most services are available. That requires a full round trip of 34.1 miles, or a more heavily traveled (but less steep) 32-mile loop back on Highway One to return to Point Arena.

OPTION 5 stays on Eureka Hill Road past the intersection at 3.1 miles, dropping moderately, then steeply to cross a bridge over the Garcia River and the San Andreas Fault at 5.1 miles, a good turnaround for moderate riders. To continue on Eureka Hill Road involves a sustained steep climb to 2320 feet at 8.8 miles, followed by a short descent, then a gradual ascent to road's end at the Point Arena Air Force Station, 10.6 miles from Highway One. The ride back features a hairy twisting descent. It's 21.2 miles round trip.

43

Point Arena Headlands

Lighthouse Road, with option on Highway One

This ride is short, but beautiful enough to enjoy on almost any day, especially when wildflowers are blooming and the sun shines. You might want to ride elsewhere when the wind is howling, or on days when the fog is thick as pea soup. For a longer ride, start from town if you don't mind doing an easy stretch of highway.

Flumeville, where this ride begins, was the site of an ingenious innovation by nineteenth century loggers. The water in a wooden flume carried lumber seven miles down the Garcia River, where it was lifted 300 feet uphill by water wheel-driven rollers to Flumeville, then hauled down to the harbor for shipping. The Point Arena Lighthouse has guided ships along this treacherous coast since 1870, although the present tower was built after the 1906 earthquake cracked the original structure.

DIRECTIONS TO STARTING POINT: North of Point Arena, turn west off Highway One at M.17.05 onto Lighthouse Road and park. (Option 3 leaves from downtown Point Arena.)

ELEVATION AT START: 175 feet

OPTION 1: Ride west on Lighthouse Road and return.
Easy, 4.6 miles round trip, light vehicle traffic.
Elevation Gain/Loss: 275 feet+/275 feet-

OPTION 2: At the west end of road, pay admission at Lighthouse and continue .4 mile. Visit the museum and climb 145 steps to the top of the lighthouse and a grand view.
Easy, 5.4 miles round trip, light vehicle traffic.
Elevation Gain/Loss: 305 feet+/305 feet-

OPTION 3: From downtown Point Arena, ride Highway One north to Light-
house Road, then do Option 1 or 2.
Easy, add 4 miles round trip, heavy vehicle traffic on highway.
Elevation Gain/Loss: Add 185 feet+/185 feet-

SURFACE: Paved county road

FEE: Admittance to Lighthouse grounds: $2.50 for adults, 50 cents for chil-
dren. Open 11–2:30 daily, 10–3:30 summer, weekends and holidays. Closed
Thanksgiving, Christmas and New Year's Day.

Ride #43

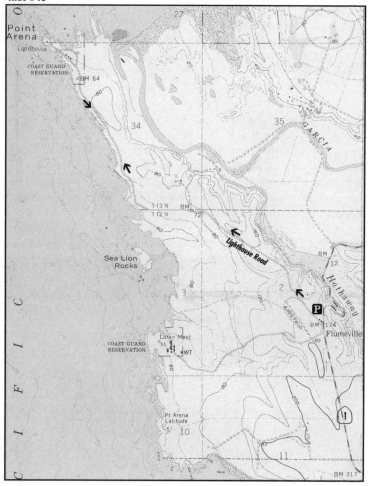

FACILITIES: Store and campground at starting point. Restrooms if you pay to enter Lighthouse grounds.

Ride Notes

Contour northwest from Highway One on occasionally bumpy Lighthouse Road. Descend briefly at .4 mile, then ascend gradually on better tread. As you top the rise at .7 mile, a 180-degree ocean vista awaits (unless its foggy). Dip and rise to a second top, then descend moderately with views of large Sea Lion Rock offshore on your left. Another stretch of bumpy tread at 1 mile precedes a short contour. Descend briefly across spectacular headlands, drawing alongside the rocky Pacific shore. After a short uphill, reach the end of the pavement at 2.2 miles, then come to the Point Arena Lighthouse entrance kiosk. Unless the Lighthouse is open, you need to turn back to complete a 4.6-mile round trip.

OPTION 2: If the Lighthouse is open, you can pay your admission and ride another .4 mile to the end of the road. Take the tour led by knowledgeable docents and climb the lighthouse for a stunning view of the western edge of the North American continent. This is the nearest the continent gets to Hawaii.

OPTION 3: For a longer ride, start from downtown Point Arena. Ascend north to the top end of Main Street. Where Highway One turns left you can continue straight one block, then go left on Lake Street and contour west to Highway One. Turn right and follow the level highway shoulder out of town. Descend slightly before coming to Lighthouse Road 2 miles from your start.

44

Ridges East of Manchester

Mountain View Road

This paved, county-maintained back road rises and dips through rugged country in one of the least settled areas of the Coast Range. The early-day stagecoach journey along this route took two days, indicating that cyclists should not take the full 25-mile shuttle lightly. Most riders will want to try one of the three shorter options, ascending to one or two of the road's several summits. Whichever choice you make, you'll get a workout.

DIRECTIONS TO STARTING POINT: Mountain View Road heads east from Highway One at M.19.34 south of Manchester.

ELEVATION AT START: 120 feet

OPTION 1: Mountain View Road to first summit.
Moderate, 7 miles round trip, light vehicle traffic.
Elevation Gain/Loss: 1250 feet+/1250 feet-

OPTION 2: Mountain View Road to second summit.
Strenuous, 11.4 miles round trip, light vehicle traffic.
Elevation Gain/Loss: 2200 feet+/2200 feet-

OPTION 3: Mountain View Road to third summit.
Strenuous, 20.2 miles round trip, light vehicle traffic.
Elevation Gain/Loss: 3080 feet+/3080 feet-

OPTION 4: Mountain View Road to Boonville.
Strenuous, 25.1 miles one way, 50.2 miles round trip, light vehicle traffic.
Elevation Gain/Loss: 4090 feet+/3710 feet- one way, 7800 feet+/7800 feet- round trip.

SURFACE: Paved county road

Ride Notes

The ride east from Highway One on broad Mountain View Road starts easy, contouring along a row of pioneer cypress trees for .4 mile. Then a moderate ascent provides a hint of steep terrain to come. By .9 mile you've gained 200 feet. Two short dips break up the ascent to 1.5 miles, where the hilltop offers sweeping ocean views across pastures. Descend steeply, rise briefly, then drop beside Brush Creek at 2.1 miles, where you cross the San Andreas Fault.

Begin a steep ascent that winds up the slope to gain a ridgetop, leaving coastal grasslands for patchy forest. The rise steepens before gaining a knob on the ridgetop at 3.5 miles. Option 1 returns from here, avoiding the long steep ascent to the east. Enjoy abundant coastal views as you drop back to Highway One, 7 miles round trip.

OPTIONS 2, 3 & 4: Mountain View Road dips 60 feet to a saddle, then

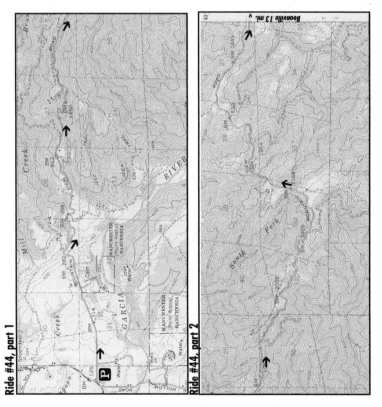

resumes a steep ascent, following the ridgetop divide between Brush Creek to the north and the Garcia River watershed to the south. Breaks in the forest on your right allow views over the wooded canyons of the Garcia. The steep rise ends at 5.2 miles. The road dips briefly, then rises to a higher ridgetop knob at 5.7 miles, 1720 feet above sea level. Option 2 turns back to complete an 11.4-mile round trip.

OPTIONS 3 & 4, for the serious road cyclist/hill lover, continue east. Mountain View Road descends to 6 miles, then resumes its steep incline, topping 2000 feet around 7 miles. Enjoy a short contour, then a fitful but gradual ascent to 8.4 miles, where a moderate climb begins. After a dip around 8.7 miles, rise steeply to the summit of Option 3 at 9.5 miles, 2250 feet. The road turns north away from the Garcia River watershed. Descend to 9.9 miles, then ascend briefly to a lesser summit at 10.1 miles. From here you have a view northeast over the headwaters of Brush Creek into the Alder Creek watershed beyond. Option 3 returns from here for a 20.2-mile round trip.

OPTION 4: If you want to negotiate more steep terrain on pavement, Mountain View Road has plenty left. You're not half way to Boonville yet and two more watersheds lay between here and road's end. The terrain eases on the next leg, a fitful descent broken by two contours. Descend moderately to a saddle at 12 miles, where the Alder Creek watershed is on your left, the Garcia still on the right. Ascend to 13 miles, then contour. Descend across a tributary of the Garcia River, then climb steadily over Hanes Ridge, passing Summit Spring near the 2000-foot summit around 17 miles.

Descend gradually, then steeply by many curves into Rancheria Creek Canyon. Drop below 500 feet to cross this pristine Navarro River tributary at 20 miles. Mountain View Road makes one final steep ascent, passing Faulkner County Park (picnicking) near the summit on Lambert Ridge before 23 miles. Descend gradually, then steeply into Anderson Valley, coming to Highway 128 at Boonville 25.1 miles from your starting point.

45

Greenwood Ridge

Greenwood Ridge Road, with options on Cameron Road & Highway One

The high rolling hills between Anderson Valley and the coast are enticing to the eye. But public access to this land of homesteads and timber tracts is limited to the few county roads that wind along the scenic ridges. Fortunately traffic on these byways is light, encouraging cycling adventures. But traffic is variable, so ride single file and stay on the right shoulder.

DIRECTIONS TO STARTING POINT: Take Greenwood Ridge Road, either east from Highway One at M.33.9 in Elk, or west from Highway 128 at M.20.15 northwest of Philo. The described rides start 2.6 miles from the coast at the junction with Cameron Road (15.5 miles from Highway 128). Park near cattle guard on Cameron Road or 200 feet up Greenwood Road at the broad dirt turnout on the right.

ELEVATION AT START: 1220 feet

OPTION 1: Greenwood Ridge Road from Cameron Road to M.5.6.
Easy, 6.2 miles round trip, light to medium vehicle traffic.
Elevation Gain/Loss: 460 feet+/460 feet-

OPTION 2: Greenwood Road to top of third big hill.
Moderate, 12.8 miles round trip, light to medium vehicle traffic.
Elevation Gain/Loss: 1230 feet+/1230 feet-

OPTION 3: Greenwood Road to Signal Ridge Road or Highway 128.
Strenuous, 23.8 or 31 miles round trip, light to medium vehicle traffic.
Elevation Gain/Loss: 2670 feet+/2670 feet- to Signal Ridge, 3960 feet+/3960 feet- to Highway 128

OPTION 4: Cameron Road, Highway One, return up Greenwood Ridge.
Strenuous, 13.8-mile loop, light to heavy vehicle traffic.
Elevation Gain/Loss: 1350 feet+/1350 feet-

SURFACE: Paved county road

FACILITIES: Only on Option 4 in Elk — store, cafes, inns.

Ride Notes

OPTIONS 1, 2 & 3: Head east on Greenwood Ridge Road, following the ridgetop route in and out of forest and through clearings of pastures and apple orchards sprinkled with homesteads. The route starts with numerous gentle ups and downs, not gaining or losing more than 50

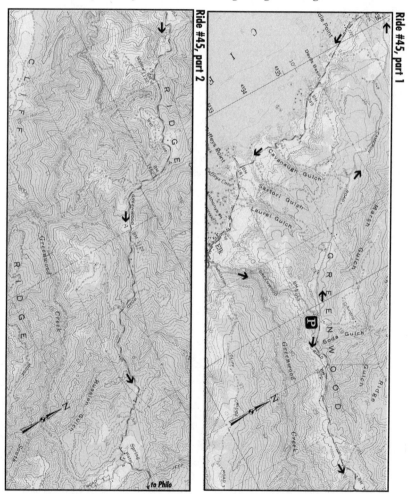

feet elevation until 2.4 miles. Then descend moderately to 2.9 miles, followed by a short ascent to 3.1 miles, where you have expansive views on the right over the deep, wooded canyon of Greenwood Creek and on the left down to the Navarro River. For the easiest ride, turn back at 2.4 or 3.1 miles. The road's terrain gets steeper to the east.

OPTIONS 2 & 3: Continue east on a moderate descent to 3.6 miles, then ascend moderately on a hill broken by a few small dips to 4.8 miles. A short descent allows a run at the steepest ascent yet, topping out at 5.4 miles. Descend slightly to 6 miles, then resume a gradual ascent to 6.4 miles, where you reach 1460 feet, the highest point so far. This is your turnaround for Option 2's moderate ride.

OPTION 3: If you continue east, a moderate descent drops 320 feet to 7.6 miles. Greenwood Ridge Road then ascends moderately to 8.1 miles, dips briefly and resumes a moderate climb to 8.6 miles. Descend moderately, then gradually past Greenwood Ridge Vineyards on a wooded section of the ridge. Ascend gradually on winding pavement to 9.8 miles, followed by a slight down and up that reaches a new high point at 10.3 miles. But the ascent on your outward leg isn't over yet. It's down, up and down to 10.7 miles. Then ascend a stiff hill to Greenwood Ridge's real summit at 11.1 miles. Here at 1530 feet, the north slope of Greenwood Ridge plunges to 80 feet elevation at the Navarro River only 1.3 miles north. Fortunately you're not heading that way. If you return from here, you avoid the 300-foot drop on the way to Signal Ridge.

Continuing east, Greenwood Ridge Road plunges steeply for .5 mile. At the bottom you pass big redwoods virtually at the headwaters of Greenwood Creek. A winding, moderate ascent comes to Signal Ridge Road (see Ride #46) at 11.9 miles, then continues to 12.1 miles. From there Greenwood Ridge Road descends steadily, sometimes precipitously for almost 3 miles. Slow for the tight turns (posted 20 mph) at 12.9 miles, and watch for glimpses of the Navarro River and the magical landscape of Anderson Valley if you choose to make the descent. Where you pass the entrances to Highland Ranch at 14.3 miles and Hendy Woods State Park at 14.9 miles, you link with Ride #38. Greenwood Ridge Road crosses the Navarro River at 15 miles and ascends briefly to end at Highway 128 at 15.5 miles.

OPTION 4: A strenuous loop from the same starting point heads northwest on Cameron Road, descending to Highway One and ending with an 1100-foot ascent on Greenwood Ridge Road. From the cattle guard at the junction, ascend gradually on Cameron Road to another cattle guard at .5 mile, then make a gentle descent along the western end of Greenwood Ridge. Drop moderately through a dip around 1.6 miles, then ascend briefly before resuming a gradual descent along the ridgetop. By 3 miles you ease down to 1000 feet elevation, a good place to turn back if you prefer an easy ramble to a strenuous loop.

From 3.2 miles the descent turns moderate. After a short up around 4 miles, descend moderately with occasional ocean views. From 5.4 miles the downhill is steep and winding until Cameron Road ends at Highway One at 5.9 miles.

Turn left on one of the most spectacular legs of scenic Highway One. Dip and rise twice to 7.1 miles, where the Devil's Basin is on your right. Dip, then contour with grand coastal views to 8 miles, then dip and rise twice through curves. Descend the crooked and treacherous Cavanaugh Grade from 8.5 to 9 miles. Contour past a field on your left, the townsite of Cuffey's Cove in the late 1800s. Ascend a short hill past the town's cemetery, then descend fitfully with some of the finest coastal vistas. Enter Elk at 10.4 miles and contour through town. At 11.2 miles, turn left on Greenwood Ridge Road and make the grueling 1100-foot ascent to your starting point.

46

Signal Ridge, Headwaters of Greenwood Creek

Signal Ridge Road, with options on Greenwood Ridge Road

The alluring high hills between Anderson Valley and the coast offer little public access, county roads being the notable exception. Signal Ridge on the northern slopes of Cold Spring Mountain offers a pleasant ride through pastures and forest, with even less traffic than you'll find on Greenwood Ridge.

DIRECTIONS TO STARTING POINT: Take Greenwood Ridge Road, either east from Highway One at M.33.9 in Elk, or west from Highway 128 at M.20.15 northwest of Philo. Signal Ridge Road is 3.6 miles from Highway 128, 14.4 miles from Elk. Park at the intersection.

ELEVATION AT START: 1300 feet

OPTION 1: Signal Ridge Road to end.
Moderate, 8.7 miles round trip, light vehicle traffic.
Elevation Gain/Loss: 1460 feet+/1460 feet-

OPTION 2: Add upper part of Greenwood Ridge Road, Ride #45.
Strenuous, add up to 12 miles or more each way, light to medium vehicle traffic.
Elevation Gain/Loss: Add 1130 feet+/1130 feet-

OPTION 3: Start from Hendy Woods or Navarro River.
Strenuous, add 6 miles round trip, light to medium vehicle traffic.
Elevation Gain/Loss: Add 1100 feet+/1100 feet-

SURFACE: Mixed paved and dirt county road

Ride Notes

After a short contour, the narrow pavement of Signal Ridge Road descends fitfully through sheep pastures to a low point beside a homestead at .5 mile, then ascends into forest. Wind through a dip around 1 mile, then ascend rough tread. The road surface is gravel with intermittent stretches of pavement from here. Come to a top at 1.5 miles, then dip and rise twice on uneven, bumpy track. Stay left at the intersection at 2.1 miles, making a winding contour to 2.7 miles broken by one moderate ascent. Climb moderately to a junction at 2.9 miles. Veer right for a short drop, then resume ascending. The mostly moderate hill has a steep climb around 3.1 miles, then reaches a top at 3.4 miles. After a short dip, ascend fitfully. Watch for a cattle guard at 3.6 miles, then rise to the top of a hill at 3.8 miles.

The next segment passes through the Rossi Ranch, prominently signed no trespassing. Continue on the winding county road, descending slightly through woods with views of the pastoral ranch. Just beyond a low point at 4 miles the road forks. The left fork ascends to the nearby top of Cold Spring Mountain, at 2736 feet the highest peak within 20 miles, but the road crosses private property. Take the county road on the right, which continues to 4.35 miles, climbing to a gate at 2180 feet. Return the way you came.

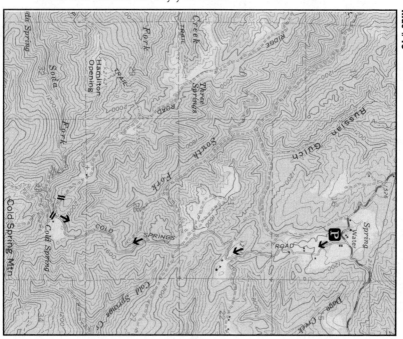

Glossary

blowdown (noun) Trees and limbs thrown in your path by a storm (not what you do on big descents).

cattle guard Did you ever hit train tracks at the wrong angle? Cattle guards are not those cow dogs that chase you away from the steers, they're like train tracks on steroids, i.e. a metal grate set in the road to discourage cattle and encourage bike wrecks.

coast (verb) To ride by force of gravity.

contour (verb) To maintain approximately the same elevation.

double track Path wide enough for two cyclists to ride parallel.

gauntlet Narrow passage lined with objects to punish those who veer off it.

landing 1. A level clearing in the forest. 2. What you do after falling.

loop A trail that returns to the place you began, if you make the correct turns.

milepost A permanent marker along road or trail that reports the distance from somewhere. Also expressed as "M.".

mogul Very short dip-bump combo that tends to make stomach float or bike fly.

roller coaster (verb) To make a series of short ups and downs.

saddle 1. Low point in a ridge connecting two higher elevations. 2. Part of the bike you want to stay in or around.

sand trap A natural device, consisting of many grains of sand, similar in purpose to artificial ones used in golf; i.e. to slow or stop momentum when you want to roll on.

schuss A straight course unimpeded by obstacles.

semi-loop Like a loop, but with an extending tangential ride, that is, out and back on the same surface.

shuttle One way ride with transportation waiting at far end (you hope).

single track Narrow path, wide enough for only one bike at a time.

skid trail/road A rough double track created by a bulldozer to drag (skid) logs from the forest (origin of "skid row").

spank To spill the cookies, whack, splat. To crash dramatically.

speed bump Obstacle in the track, placed intentionally or accidentally, to slow you down.

tank trap A water bar on steroids, used in attempts to prevent four-wheelers, tanks and other off-road motor vehicles from proceeding further along a route.

walk (verb) A primitive means of locomotion using the feet on the ground, one in front of the other, used by conscientious cyclists to get around mudholes without tearing up the track. Also used to ascend steep hills by those with less muscle or lung power than superbiker.

water bar Not where you fill your canteen — a drainage trench of varying depth cutting diagonally across road or trail, with a raised berm on the downhill side.

Bike Shops in Mendocino County

(Area code 707)

ON THE COAST

Catch-a-Canoe & Bicycles, Too!
937-0273
At The Stanford Inn By The Sea
Coast Highway One and Comptche-
Ukiah Road
P. O. Box 487, Mendocino 95460
Open daily for rentals, service, sales

Fort Bragg Cyclery
964-3509
579 South Franklin St.
Fort Bragg 95437
Open Monday through Saturday for rentals, service, sales

Ocean Trail
964-1260
1260 North Main Street, B-4
Fort Bragg 95437
Open daily for rentals, service, sales

Adventure Rents
884-4386
Behind the Gualala Hotel
Gualala 95445
On call anytime, rentals, sales

INLAND

Suncycles
459-2453
151 North Main St., Willits 95490
Open Monday through Saturday for service, sales

The Bike Shop/ Earthlab Energy Systems
459-3696
358 South Main St., Willits 95490
Open Tuesday through Saturday for service, sales

Dave's Bike Shop
462-3230
846 South State St., Ukiah 95482
Open Monday through Saturday for service, sales

Ukiah Schwinn Center
462-2686
178 East Gobbi St., Ukiah 95482
Open Monday through Saturday for service, sales

Mendocino Coast Cycling Events

Tour de Skunk
Mid-May and mid-October
964-6371

You and your mountain bike start the day with a train ride on the California Western (Skunk) Railroad from Fort Bragg, then ride 26 miles back to town, partly across private property.
    Benefits Mendocino Coast Recreation & Park District.

North Coast AIDS Walk & Bike Ride
Sunday before Memorial Day
961-1920

Enjoy a 10- or 22-mile mountain bike ride along Big River and raise money for AIDS research at the same time.
    Benefits ACCESS.

Important phone numbers

(Area Code 707)

Jackson State Forest 964-5674

Mendocino Area State Parks 937-5804

Sinkyone Wilderness State Park 986-7711

Mendocino County Road Department 463-4363

Bureau of Land Management 468-4000

Ft Bragg-Mendocino Chamber of Commerce 961-6300, 800/726-2780

Bored Feet Publications 964-6629

ABOUT BORED FEET

We began Bored Feet Publications in 1986 to publish and distribute *The Hiker's hip pocket Guide to the Mendocino Coast*. Our publishing company has grown by presenting the most accurate guide books for northern California.

We like to hear your feedback about our products! And if you would like to receive updates on trails we cover in our publications, send us your name and address, specifying your counties of interest.

We also offer FLEET FEET BOOKS, our lightning-fast mail order service offering books and maps about northern California. Your purchases directly from Bored Feet support our independent publishing efforts to bring you more information about the spectacularly scenic North Coast of California. Thanks for your support!

If you would like more of our guides please send check or money order, adding $3 shipping for orders under $25, $5 over $25 ($5/7 for rush).

THE ONLY COMPREHENSIVE GUIDES TO THE NORTH COAST:

Hiker's hip pocket Guide to Sonoma County	$14.00
Hiker's hip pocket Guide to the Humboldt Coast	13.00
Hiker's hip pocket Guide to the Mendocino Coast	13.00
Hiker's hip pocket Guide to the Mendocino Highlands	13.95
Boxed Gift Set: Mendocino Coast, Humboldt Coast, Sonoma	37.00
Great Day Hikes in & around Napa Valley	11.00
Mendocino Coast Bike Rides	12.00
A Tour of Mendocino: 32 Historic Buildings	6.00
Trails of the Lost Coast Map	5.95
Yolla Bolly-Middle Eel Wilderness Trail Map	5.95
Glove Box Guide: Mendocino Coast: Lodgings, Eateries, Sights, History, Activities & More	11.00

For shipping to a California address, please add 7.25% tax.
PRICES SUBJECT TO CHANGE WITHOUT NOTICE

BORED FEET · P.O.Box 1832, Mendocino, CA 95460 · 707/ 964-6629